DIGGING FOR VICTORY

V DIGGING *for* ICTORY

WARTIME GARDENING WITH MR MIDDLETON

C.H. Middleton

First published in this new edition
2008 by Aurum Press Ltd
7 Greenland Street
London NW1 0ND
www.aurumpress.co.uk

First published in 1942 by George Allen & Unwin Ltd

A catalogue record for this book is available from the British
Library.

ISBN 978 1 84513 371 9

1 3 5 7 9 10 8 6 4 2
2008 2010 2012 2011 2009

Printed in Great Britain by MPG Books, Bodmin, Cornwall

PREFACE

I SEEM to have been talking about gardens and gardening for a very long time, and have added many grey hairs to my scanty crop since I first faced a microphone. But it has been a pleasant experience, and has brought me many friends. In happier days we talked of rock gardens, herbaceous borders, and verdant lawns; but with the advent of war and its grim demands, these pleasant features rapidly receded into the background to make way for the all-important food crops.

But interest in the garden has never slackened; it has, if anything, been intensified by the urgent necessity of growing food, and presumably most of my old friends still listen when I hold forth on Leeks, Lettuces, and Leatherjackets, instead of Lilac, Lilies, and Lavender; while many who are unable to listen have paid me the compliment of asking for copies of the talks. So here is another selection of them, covering the period from September (when I usually start the new series) round to May. Very practical stuff, I'm afraid, and largely spade-work; but I hope you will find them helpful and of sufficient interest to enable you to read them without boredom. These are critical times, but we shall get through them, and the harder we dig for victory the sooner will the roses be with us again.

C. H. M.

July 1942

CONTENTS

September

TAKING STOCK

THE summer seems to be slipping away rather quickly, it is a long time coming, and it doesn't remain with us very long. It has been a patchy sort of season this year, but I suppose it might have been worse. We mopped our brows and complained about the heat in June, then put our winter undies on again in July and moaned about the wet and the cold, but take it all round we seem to have managed quite well and the gardens and allotments are not looking at all bad.

I suppose I ought to start with a few apologies, especially to listeners who have written me nice letters and have received no reply. It must be rather annoying to write a letter about some urgent gardening problem, and get back a mere formal acknowledgment or nothing at all, and I'm afraid some of you are scarcely on speaking terms with me now. But honestly I do my best, but if I devoted the whole of my time to answering letters I couldn't do justice to the numbers that arrive by every post, and actually I have very little spare time at all. Since I was here in the spring I have been running about the country giving lectures and one thing and another, often to come back and find an accumulation of work which was just a little bit too much for me. So if I haven't answered your letter please be a sport and forgive me, and don't put it down to slackness or lack of interest, will you?

How is the garden looking, anyway? I hope you have all had a successful season, with not too many disappointments. There's one thing, we haven't had to do a great deal of watering. Early in July it got very dry in my garden, but I don't like watering, so I put it off till the things were absolutely parched, then I spent a whole

evening carrying water, and before the morning it rained!
That was St. Swithin's Day, when the little apples are supposed to be christened, and they say if it rains on that day
it rains for forty days, and St. Swithin certainly did his
best not to let the old people down this year. Most of my
stuff was on the late side, but I don't know that it was any
the worse for that. We have never been without a fresh
vegetable of some kind. It is a rather remarkable thing,
and something to be very thankful for when you come to
think of it, that our cultivated vegetables can be so conveniently spread over the whole year; it would be very
awkward if all the crops turned in together and we had to
gather and harvest everything in the autumn. I don't
think I ever appreciated spring cabbages so much as this
year; we had to wait for them owing to the cold spring,
but they were good when they did arrive. Those first spring
cabbages are very sweet and tasty, especially if you can get
a nice young duck to go with them, or a bit of boiled home-
cured ham. I tried out half a dozen popular varieties of
cabbages, just to find out which suited the district best,
and when they were ready they were all good, but I'm
bothered if I could tell one from the other. All the seedsmen seem to have their own particular pet, and there must
be scores of them, but I believe you could reduce them all
to about half a dozen groups and very few people would
be able to sort them out. That, of course, applies to a good
many other vegetables too, but I don't know that it
matters, so long as they are all good—it gives the
gardeners something to argue about. The cabbages were
like the wall-flowers this year, they hung about a bit too
long and got in the way of the later crops. I like to finish
them up by the middle of June, but this year we were
cutting them in July. If I were a breeder of spring cabbages I should be inclined to concentrate on earliness, it
seems rather important in their case, though in a general

way I don't agree with the usual craze for getting things early. I certainly haven't had things too early this year. I didn't cut a decent marrow till the middle of August. The plants stood still for a long time, and got very dry, then, just before the rain came I gave them a tonic, and within a fortnight they were trying to get over the fence into the next garden, and some of them were half-way up the apple tree. I've got a few good ones now, and hope to get a nice pair for our local show next week, and I hope to have two or three good big ones to get ripe, and hang them up for the winter; we may be glad of them then. Onions seem plentiful, but the crops vary a good deal in different parts of the country; mine are good, and all they want now is a bit more nice weather to ripen them ready for harvesting. I bought a box of Ailsa Craig and Premier, and planted them out, and also sowed a dozen rows of Bedfordshire Champion, and I gave them all a nice little dose of chicken manure and a dressing of general fertilizer. Just before sowing I gave a sprinkling of bone meal, and I should think every seed must have germinated. I kept thinning and thinning, and I've never eaten so many spring onions in my life—I couldn't go near anybody for weeks—and when the shops were charging a penny each for them, I was giving them away wholesale. I could have made quite a lot of money if I'd had sense enough. I am a great believer in thinning, as a rule, to prevent overcrowding, but I don't believe in being too drastic with onions unless, of course, I want big specimens for show. My Bedfordshire Champions were left fairly close, and now they are practically touching each other and are about the size of billiard balls, but they are lovely little onions, and ripening well, and plenty of them, and for my part I would rather have a dozen medium or small onions than half a dozen double the size. I can see no advantage in getting large ones if you can get the same weight in a greater number of smaller ones. My transplanted Ailsa Craigs are very much on the large side, but I am hoping to pick out a dozen good ones for the show, though I doubt whether they will keep as well as the smaller ones—overfed onions rarely keep well.

You might not think it but I'm getting quite excited over our village show next Saturday. I've had a good deal to do with shows in recent years, but it is a very rare thing for me to show anything myself, and I'm getting quite a thrill out of it. With a bit of luck I might win a nice set of carvers, although I don't know what I'm going to carve with them if I get them, or perhaps a tin of fertilizer or a gardening book, or half a crown, so I go out every morning and look at the onions and measure the runner beans, and see if the tomatoes are colouring up. It will take them all their time to do it, but you never know. There is something extremely satisfying about winning a prize at a show. Apart from that there is something very interesting and pleasant about the atmosphere of a local flower show. It reminds us of the good old days. It brings the gardening fraternity and the allotment holders together, and keeps the gardening interest alive. There will be a good many arguments in our local before this time next week if I know anything about it. We chose the 13th for our show because we thought it might be lucky for once and bring us a fine day. We are holding it in the grounds of the local mansion, complete with flags, jangles and wangles. We are having a band, a few speeches, dart competitions, bowling for a pig, and all the rest of it. We are determined to have one day off from Hitlerism if we can possibly manage it, and I hope we shall be able to send a nice little contribution to the Red Cross. If you like to listen in next Saturday afternoon you might hear us, and I'll tell you if I've won anything. You may think mid-September rather late to hold a show, most places prefer them in July or early August. I have been to a good many during the past five or six weeks, and July, with the nice long evenings, is the ideal month for peace-time flower shows. But this is war and the war-time show is, or should be, an important item in the Dig for Victory campaign.

We are out to produce all the good food we can and to encourage better methods of using it, so we are having classes for cookery, preserving and so on, and we have chosen the season when most of the good things are available, with the object of avoiding waste in any shape or form. To hold a vegetable show in July means that an enthusiastic exhibitor may dig up several rows of potatoes or carrots just to find a dozen good ones. We are not out to encourage that sort of thing now, we would rather wait till the normal season of harvest, when there is plenty to choose from, even though it may mean cutting it a bit short to get home before the blackout. With the same end in view we are not including classes for some of the winter vegetables. I was judging at a show over a month ago and got into bad odour with one or two of the exhibitors because I didn't give first prizes to collections containing parsnips, celery and brussels sprouts, but surely nobody wants such vegetables in the middle of summer and to push them on early just for a show is a form of waste not to be encouraged in war-time, at least that is how I feel about it. But I'm afraid I am drifting away from the garden proper. At one time I was afraid the potatoes were going to be very light owing to the early dry weather and I expected to see a good deal of second growth. Then the heavy rains came and I began to get the wind up about blight, but I have been pleasantly surprised. The early ones, Sharpe's Express, were a fair crop, but the quality was poor, they seemed firmer and drier than usual. Majestics are quite good, but nothing to sing a song about; Arran Banner has produced the heaviest crop, I have just

lifted a root to have a look at them and found eight good
potatoes. I've seen better crops, but if my little lot is a fair
average for the whole country we shan't have done so
badly. I think peas have been good in a general way. Mine
were a bit disappointing. I only planted three rows,
"Gradus," "Little Marvel," and "Peter Pan." During the
dry weather I watched them and pinched them day after
day to see if there was anything in them, then they seemed
to come all of a sudden and we had so many we had to
give them away and a fortnight later we had none at all.
Just bad management, of course; I ought to have had a
row or two of later varieties. Some of my friends did and
they are still gathering them. Most of the other things are
well up to average; the green stuff looks fairly well and we
shall have enough parsnips and carrots and a nice row of
swedes, so take it all round I'm not grousing. I notice that
the brussels sprouts have grown a bit soft and top-heavy
owing to the August rains, so I am pulling the soil up to
them with the hoe; this encourages new roots to come from
the stems and the plants get extra anchorage to hold them
firm. Perhaps the less said about fruit crops the better. I
can only hope that most parts of the country are better off
than we are. We have had a fair quantity of gooseberries
and red currants, but precious little else. The strawberries
let us down badly, there were only about a dozen and they
weren't up to much. We didn't get enough black currants
on a dozen bushes to make a pot of jam. Plums were a
washout too, there may be enough late ones to make a tart
if we can find the sugar and that's about all. Apples are
about half a crop and they are my greatest disappointment.
I can do without most of the soft fruits, but I do like a
crop of apples. I think I am well below the average, which
is one consolation, some of my friends seem to have fared
better and I hope you have.

Well, I'm afraid I've talked for a quarter of an hour

about little or nothing, but it's interesting sometimes to look back over the season and count the gains and losses, but we mustn't do too much looking back. We must look forward and put our backs into it, for there is going to be plenty of work in the garden during the next month or two and during the coming Sundays we shall have to get down to brass tacks, whatever they may be, and discuss ways and means of increasing production. Take it all round this has been a fairly good year. We must try to make next year a better one still.

POTATOES, BUGS AND OTHER THINGS

I wonder how many of you have sprayed your potatoes this year? I'm afraid we didn't get much suitable weather for the job after early July, and a good many of the crops must have been missed. It's no use talking about it now, of course, I only mention it because I was looking over some allotments the other day and saw an excellent example of the good results of spraying. I wish you could have seen it—a plot which was sprayed twice was standing as green and fresh as ever, while others round about it which hadn't been sprayed looked almost as brown as if they had been given a dose of weed killer. I think many people regard it as a natural process that potato foliage should turn brown and die in September, but it shouldn't. It should still be green, at least the late varieties should, and would be if they were kept free from the disease, and when you see a plot which has been kept clean it is a very convincing proof of the value of spraying. Some of my allotments friends are now busy cutting off the foliage in the mistaken belief that it will prevent the disease spreading to the tubers, but I'm afraid I am not very hopeful about it, handling the diseased foliage scatters thousands of spores all over the soil and they soon find their way down below—especially when it rains. This year, cutting the foliage may have one advantage. The foliage everywhere is very heavy and keeps the soil wet underneath, so if it is out of the way, the sun can have a chance to dry the ground a bit. In any case, the potatoes won't grow any more without the tops, so my advice is lift the entire crop as soon as possible, leave them out in the air to dry for a time, and dust them over with powdered lime before putting them under cover—we shall be dealing with the question of storing for winter in a later talk.

With the exception of some of the late varieties, potatoes won't improve in the ground, either in quantity or quality, so I hope to get all mine up during the next fortnight. Then I shall sow a green crop on the ground for digging in as manure in the spring. My onions are ripening nicely, and I hope to get them all under cover before this month is out. The harvesting of onions is important if you want to keep them through the winter. The tops should be dying down now, so it is a good plan to lift the onions half out of the ground by putting a fork under them. Leave them like that for a few days and then pull them out altogether. Leave them on the ground for a day or two, or if you can manage it, spread them out on a frame of wire netting above the ground so that the air can get round them and the sun can get at them to warm and ripen them. If you can protect them from the rain so much the better, and they should be left like this till every bit of green has gone from the stems, when they will be ready for storing. Sounds a bit of trouble perhaps, but it doesn't take long, and after all, we made enough fuss about sowing them and growing them, so we may as well finish the job by harvesting them properly. I had a nice row of White Lisbon onions which were sown last year and planted out in the spring, and I thought I was going to get a few fine specimens, but for some reason or other they have nearly all split into two halves. I think they got very dry during the early summer, and then heavy rains, plus a dose of fertilizer, made them swell too quickly, and instead of making nice solid bulbs, they cracked up, and some of them went to seed. It's no use trying to keep any of them, so we are using them up now. Something similar happened to my outdoor tomatoes; they started off very nicely and set the first trusses of fruit, then got dry while I was away and came more or less to a standstill. When I could get at them I picked all the side shoots out, gave them a dose of fertilizer, perhaps a little too much, and a thorough soaking; the result was that every tomato which had reached any size, instead of growing bigger, cracked their skins as they ripened, and were hardly worth gathering. I have had some good ones since and there are any amount of green ones now which I hope will ripen. The lesson to be learnt from this is that the watering and feeding of tomatoes should be a regular operation, not spasmodic; to leave them for a long period till they are half starved and dry and the skins of the fruits and the stems are tough, and then give them a heavy meal, causes a sudden rush of sap which bursts the skins and produces fat young shoots all over the top of the plant, instead of nice steady growth and bunches of healthy fruit. A little weak liquid manure twice a week is far better than a heavy dose once a fortnight, and that applies, not only to tomatoes, but to all the other growing crops. We should aim at maintaining a steady growth and avoid sudden jumps and jerks. Tomatoes at this time of the year should be gathered as soon as they begin to change colour, they ripen quite well indoors and the later ones get a better chance.

I have noticed a good many white butterflies about and you know what that means—caterpillars on the brussels and other greens if something isn't done about it. I find a tennis racket a very good thing for swatting white butterflies. I'm getting quite expert at it and developing quite a good overarm stroke, but even so, you can't swat them all and they still find their way to the cabbage leaves, so I usually have a look through the plants to find their eggs. These are laid in clusters and stuck to the undersides of the leaves; they are bright yellow and easy to see, and if you squash them with your thumb and finger that means one colony of caterpillars less. When you are looking for these eggs it pays to look carefully because there is a little fly, known as ichneumon, which preys on the cabbage caterpillars and kills them; it is, therefore, a good friend and worth preserving. This little fly spins itself up into a cocoon and sticks to a cabbage leaf, and there are usually several of them clustered together, and being yellow they are easily mistaken, at first sight, for the eggs of the white butterfly. The cocoons, however, are rough and woolly, while the eggs are smooth and shiny. If we could breed enough of these ichneumon flies we shouldn't be troubled with caterpillars, but then, I suppose, if there were no caterpillars the flies would die of starvation, so we can't have it both ways. I usually dust the greens over about once a week with derris powder. I've got one of those little puffers with a tin on the end which you fill with the powder and it doesn't take many minutes to puff it about through the plants, and if you do it regularly from now on you won't be troubled much by caterpillars, nor by that wretched little white fly which sometimes makes such a mess of the brussels sprouts, but it's no use waiting till the flies rise in clouds every time you disturb the plants, you must get there first and keep them away.

Talking about caterpillars reminds me of those wicked little green ones which sometimes chew the apple tree leaves all to ribbons in the spring. These are the caterpillars of the winter moth, a little brown moth which is now in the mating season and is about to start laying eggs on the apple twigs ready to hatch out into caterpillars in the spring. The lady moth of this species is unable to fly, her wings are not big enough, so when she has finished her honeymoon she crawls up the apple tree and lays her eggs on the twigs at the base of the buds; then she dies, but in the spring the eggs hatch out into caterpillars just when the young leaves are opening out, and there is their breakfast all ready for them. One of the methods of stopping this little game is to put grease bands on the trees now. These consist of paper bands tied round the trunk of the tree about six feet above the ground, and smeared over with one of the grease banding materials which you can buy in tins specially for this purpose. It is a sticky bird-lime substance, after the manner of a fly-paper, and when Mrs. Moth starts on her journey up the tree she puts her foot into it and gets no further. I don't know whether you can get the paper this year, I'm afraid it is likely to be scarce. I couldn't get it last year, so I painted a band round the tree with white lead paint, let it get dry, and then smeared a narrow ribbon of the grease on the paint. It caught quite a lot of thieving insects and so far as I can tell has not made the slightest difference to the tree. We are told not to put the grease directly on to the bark, and certainly the paper is much nicer and less messy, but I don't suppose it would do any harm just for once, especially if you paint it first. Whichever way you do it, do it now—if you leave it till later you will miss quite a lot of moths.

I have had a couple of busy evenings this week with the secateurs pruning raspberries and rambler roses. This is a job which ought to be done without further delay so that the young canes can get the benefit of the rest of the summer to ripen and mature them ready for next year's crop. Pruning raspberries is a very simple job. You merely cut out all the old canes which have borne the fruit to make room for the new ones which have grown this year, right down to the ground and burn them, because there may be various insect pests in them which, if left in peace, will carry on the breed to next year. Then you select the strongest of the young ones to take their places and cut down all the surplus ones if there are too many to fill the row, unless, of course, you want some new ones for planting somewhere else; if you do you must leave them another month or so and then dig them out complete with roots. The usual way with raspberries is to tie the canes to a horizontal wire, or perhaps two, one above the other, stretched immediately over the plants. I find a better way is to put the plants, not under the wires, but along the side, about eighteen inches away from them, then you can pull over the young canes and tie them to the wires about six inches apart all along them. In the summer these canes will fruit, while the young ones grow up well away from the wires instead of being all crowded together. After fruiting it is then a simple matter to cut off the old canes and clear the wires and pull over and tie up the new ones for next year. Don't cut the tops off the young canes now, March is the time to do that. And don't prune the autumn fruiting varieties now, such as "Hailsham Berry" and "November Abundance." These are cut down in the spring and fruit in the autumn on canes which have grown during the summer. Rambler roses are pruned on exactly the same principle; by cutting out the old canes or branches which have borne this year's flowers, and training into their places those long green ones which have been growing up from the bottom during the summer, because these will give you the best flowers next year. Cut the old ones as low down as you can. If there are enough young ones springing direct from the base so much the better, if not select those as low down on the old stems as possible and cut the old ones off just above them. Mind you, this only applies to the true ramblers, such as Dorothy Perkins, Crimson Rambler, American Pillar, and so on. The climbing hybrid tea roses, such as climbing General Mac-Arthur, which are merely climbing forms of the ordinary hybrid tea, should not be pruned now—March is the time for them. Black currants, too, if you haven't already pruned them, should be attended to at once, on the same principle as the ramblers, by cutting out the old wood and leaving a bush of young shoots which have grown this summer.

GATHERING IN THE HARVEST

I hope you have all got some nice crops of potatoes and other good things for the winter store. The time has come now when we must take stock of the harvest and make sure that it is gathered and put away in good condition. We are sometimes apt to be a little careless at this time of the year, when supplies are abundant, and it is easy to waste good food, which ought to carry us well into the winter, for the want of a little extra care in harvesting. We have all worked pretty hard this year to get good crops, so don't let us spoil the ship for the sake of a penn'orth of tar; let us see to it that everything worth keeping is gathered into the store. How are you going to store your potatoes, for instance? In country districts where there are plenty of barns and cellars available it isn't much of a problem, but in the modern homes of urban districts storage accommodation is sometimes very limited and the new allotment holder may be wondering what to do with his potatoes and other root crops. Now it doesn't matter where you store potatoes so long as you can provide certain essential conditions for them which are really not difficult at all. In the first place they should be well harvested and dried, if possible, before putting them away. If you put them away wet all sorts of unpleasant things are likely to happen and half of them may go rotten. Try to select nice fine weather for lifting. I know that is sometimes easier said than done, but I think we are entitled to expect a few fine dry days this month. You can't lift potatoes successfully when the ground is wet and muddy, the ideal condition is when the soil is moderately dry and the potatoes roll out clean and free from soil. If you can leave them spread out on the ground for about half a day in a nice sunny breeze so much the better, but you mustn't leave them out in the sun for more than a day or it will turn them green and bitter. If you can put them inside a shed or airy building of some sort lightly covered with straw or similar material to keep the light, but not the air, away from them for about a fortnight, they will be in good condition for storing. This waiting period may not be absolutely essential in all cases but it is a decided advantage, because potatoes perspire rather freely for a time after lifting and if there is not sufficient air among them during this period they get sweaty and hot and that soon leads to trouble. I have known amateurs to lift them and put them straight into a pit or clamp and almost seal them over with soil so that very little air could get to them, and in a fortnight's time, when they were examined, they were positively hot and steamy, setting up the same sort of spontaneous combustion that you sometimes see in a hay-rick which was not properly dried—then, of course, they soon go bad. So careful harvesting and moderate drying is one of the first principles—the rest is comparatively easy. A cool cellar or shed, a corner in an old dark barn, or any similar place does quite well provided it is frost-proof. Potatoes like to be kept cool, the cooler the better, and a little straw or bracken, or a few old sacks thrown over them, will keep out several degrees of frost. The worst place to put them is in a wooden loft or a spare bedroom where the atmosphere is very dry and sometimes warm, the tubers soon shrivel and sprout under such conditions, so keep them cool. They mustn't be frozen, of course, being such tropical creatures, but they can get within a few degrees of it quite safely. The next point is darkness. Potatoes in store must not be exposed to daylight; the potatoes themselves wouldn't mind it, but the light would turn them green and make the skins thick and bitter so that you couldn't eat them. If you are saving some for seed it doesn't matter about the light, in fact it makes them tough and they keep better, but eating potatoes must be kept in the dark. They must also have ventilation because they are alive and breathing, particularly for a month or two after lifting; in the dead of winter they don't need so much but even then they must never be completely shut up in airtight places. For those who have no room under cover for them the clamp or pit is the best method of storing. It is an old country way of doing it, but it still takes a bit of beating. You can make a clamp in any out-of-the-way corner of the garden, but the ideal place is on the north side of a wall or fence away from the sun. Clear a piece of ground, say about three feet wide and as long as you like, put down a layer of ashes or cinders and then stack the potatoes on this in a ride-shaped heap about eighteen inches or two feet high, not more. I know one gardener who always puts a thin faggot of brushwood along the middle, and builds the potatoes over it; this provides an air channel underneath them and is quite a sound idea. If you can get a barrowload of fine coke breeze to throw over them it will prevent them sprouting in the early spring, but don't do that with seed potatoes. After stacking, cover the heap with a thick layer of straw, or rough grass or bracken, thoroughly dried, will do. Straw is the best and don't just flop it on anyhow, take a little trouble with it and comb it out if you can, so that the straws are all in one direction, up and down the heap, not across it. The idea is to make a sort of thatch such as you see on hayricks or country cottages, and you should pack it as close as possible and make it at least nine inches thick. Then you dig a trench all round the heap, plastering the soil from it over the straw about four inches thick and smoothing it down with a spade to form a sort of pie crust or roof; make the sides fairly steep and then the winter rain will run off it into the trench and the potatoes will remain high and dry and comfortable. There is just one other thing, ventilation, and this is most important. Here and there along the top you must fix twisted wisps of straw through the soil or sloping drainpipes, or anything which your own ingenuity may suggest, to let a certain amount of air in and out without letting the rain or frost get in. Country people use the twists of straw about a yard apart and they answer very well. That, then, is a clamp, and you can also store carrots, beets, swedes, and any other of the root crops by this method and they will keep quite well. The only snag is that you can't very well put them all in one clamp because of the inconvenience of getting at them as and when required. I usually put potatoes at one end and parsnips or swedes at the other because they won't be wanted much till after Christmas. But there is no need to lift either parsnips or swedes for another month yet, or even then, unless you want the ground; parsnips are natives and can stop out all the winter without harm if need be—they even improve in flavour by getting frozen. I store beetroots and carrots in a very simple way. I make a sort of wooden bin on the concrete at the back of the house, stack the roots loosely in it, cover them layer by layer with finely sifted sandy soil till the whole heap is well covered, an old sack or two over the top and a couple of sheets of corrugated iron to keep the wet out. Then when we want a few we just lift off the covering and dive into the soil, like having a dip in the old bran tub, and get what we require. They keep in perfect condition like that. I don't store the stump-rooted carrots at all; the last bed of these was sown at the end of July and we shall keep pulling them as they get big enough, and with ordinary luck they ought to last till Christmas and then we start on the stored ones. You can, of course, store them all as the ground is needed, but the little ones are much sweeter freshly pulled from the bed.

I mentioned seed potatoes a few minutes ago. I don't know whether you are saving any of your own, I don't usually recommend it, but we are doing a lot of things now that we don't normally do, and if you've got a good healthy crop there is no reason why you shouldn't save a few, just to be on the safe side. But if you do save some, don't lift the entire crop and then pick out the small ones for seed; that is the wrong way to do it because many of them may be small because the plant was unhealthy, perhaps suffering from one of the mysterious virus diseases, and you don't want to perpetuate that. The best way to save seed is to do it at lifting time, in fact it ought to have been done earlier, but it's no use talking about that now. Instead of picking out the small potatoes, keep a weather eye open for an extra good plant with a good clean crop on it, then pick out the smaller ones from that and put them on one side. When you've got enough put them in flat trays or boxes and leave them outside in the shade for a week or two, but cover them up if it rains; then you can put them on a shelf in the shed or some convenient cool place and they will keep quite well through the winter.

The onion crop is worth a little trouble too. We made a good deal of fuss about them when there were none to be had, so we may as well take care of them now that we have a few. We have already discussed the ripening and harvesting process, so I hope they are ready now for the winter store. I think the first requirement of onions in store is a good circulation of fresh air; they don't mind being cold, they will even stand a degree or two of frost—what they will not tolerate is a damp, close atmosphere. A dry shed or a loft or attic is just right so long as it is not too warm. The old country idea is to tie them to short lengths of rope or sticks and hang them up to the rafters, and there is a lot to be said for it; it may seem a bit tedious, but it doesn't take so long as you might think once you get the idea right. You start at the bottom of the rope or stick and bind the onions in one above the other all round it. I find rough sticks selected from the old pea boughs are the best, with a few notches on them to prevent the top onions slipping down. I use the sticks with the thick end upwards, so that I can cut them off at a strong side branch and leave a bit of it on to form a hook to hang the stick up with. The advantages of this hanging up method are that the onions are all open to the air and to the eye, and they occupy no floor space, which is a great consideration where space is limited. They will even finish their ripening process there if you haven't been able to finish them off out of doors.

And what about those haricot beans you have all been growing for the winter store? They should all be pulled up now and hung upside down in bunches in the sun if possible, but protected from the rain, until the foliage is quite yellow and dead, and the beans in the pods are hard and dry. Then you can shell them out and put them away for the winter. They keep best in a linen bag or a small sack so that a little air can get to them. I saw some stored last year in biscuit tins with close fitting lids which kept them more or less airtight, and they went mouldy. It may have been because they were not thoroughly ripe and dry before they were put away, but it's just as well to be on the safe side. The same applies to peas, they ought to be hard and dry and yellow before they are finally put away.

Finally, there are those winter marrows. There are

plenty of big ones about, but it hasn't been too good a year for ripening them. They ought to be hung up or put on a wire frame or something in the sun till they are quite hard and every vestige of green has gone. It is even worth while to take them in at night and put them out during the day for a week or two, because the nights are beginning to get cold and damp. When you are satisfied that they are quite ripe, hang them up to the beams in the kitchen or any convenient place with a piece of old fish netting or with strings, and they will keep well into the winter. You can have a look at them now and then, and if you see any soft spots appearing use them up at once, but I have kept them till well into the New Year, and they came in very useful as a winter dish, and may be even more acceptable this year.

Don't waste anything for the sake of a little trouble in harvesting and keeping it.

PREPARING FOR THE WINTER

The evenings are drawing in now and we shall have to be prepared for Jack Frost and get the tender plants under cover before the nights get too cold. I'm afraid we haven't had a very brave show of flowers this year, and they may get scarcer still as time goes on so we may as well take care of those we have. I have a few oddments about the place which I should like to keep—a few special dahlias, some fuchsias, and some of those old-fashioned geraniums with brightly coloured leaves which you don't see very often nowadays. The difficulty is to know where to put them; even if you have a little greenhouse you don't want to clutter it up with dead-looking plants, so I'm going to try a very old-fashioned dodge with mine. I tried it last year, and although I lost a few, the majority kept alive and blossomed forth again in the spring. I dig them up about

27

this time, the geraniums and fuchsias, I mean, and a few heliotropes and cram them altogether in some boxes of soil, leaving them outside as long as I can, putting them in the shed on frosty nights—I give them one watering and then no more. When they are quite faded and dry I wrap the roots up in sacking, not singly, but in bundles, and hang them up in the shed, where they remain till early March. Then I cut them back rather severely, pot them up, and put them in the greenhouse. They soon begin to sprout out and make new growth. I take cuttings then from the fuchsias and heliotropes and throw the old plants away; I find the cuttings make the best flowering plants for the summer, but sometimes the old plants also make fine specimens, and with care you can keep them for years. I don't say this is the best way to winter them—a greenhouse is better—but this answers very well when space is limited. The dahlias I dig up just as they are, pack them together on the floor in the stable, cover the roots with soil, and leave them there quite dry to sleep till the spring. I had a few of the bright scarlet salvia splendens, which is a very attractive plant, and also a row of the small-flowered begonia sempervirens. I expect most of you know it, rather fleshy leaves and small pink or red flowers—a pretty and very tidy plant, commonly used for edging. The snag about these begonias, and also the scarlet salvias, is they just get into their stride, as it were, when the frost comes and cuts them down, because they are both tender; but you can enjoy their beauty for another month or two yet if you lift them carefully, pot them up and bring them indoors. Just trim them up a bit and pick off the old flowers and they will keep flowering for some time to come. I have done this, too, with the annual carnations which are usually a mass of buds in the Autumn, but just fizzle away because of the cold nights. In pots in a cool greenhouse they will keep on flowering into the winter, but you must lift them carefully, disturb the roots as little as possible, and pick off all the flowers which are open.

Chrysanthemums which have been out of doors all the summer should also be brought indoors to flower now. I expect most of the small greenhouses have been full of tomatoes all the summer, but they are getting a bit weary-looking now, and not likely to produce much more, so I should pick all the tomatoes off, and hang them up in bunches, or put them in boxes to ripen; then you can take out the old plants, clean the house down and have a few flowers in it.

Tomatoes out of doors won't do any more good now, so you may as well gather them all, green or otherwise, and take them indoors—some of them will ripen, and the others are useful for making chutney. There are several ways of ripening green tomatoes; some put them between layers of flannel in a box—my mother always did that, and put them in a dark cupboard, and she used to make them last nearly up to Christmas; some pack them in sawdust, or put them on shelves in the greenhouse, or along the window ledge, and they all claim theirs to be the best and only way to do it. Actually, I don't think it matters much—warmth is the most important factor; if a tomato has passed a certain stage it will finish the ripening process in any warm corner, light or dark. I really believe they do it better in the dark though I shouldn't like to explain why. While we are on the harvesting and storing question, have you ever tried lifting runner beans and keeping the roots? If you dig them up when the frost cuts the tops, cut off the stems a foot above the ground and store the roots in soil in an out-building just as you do with the dahlias—they keep quite well, in fact, they often have tubers on the roots very much like the dahlias. They keep well so long as they are quite dry and frost-proof, and you can plant them out again towards the end of April. I don't know that you will get better crops from them in the second year, than you do from seed—not quite such fine beans, perhaps, but you get them considerably earlier, as much as three weeks sometimes, and this year, in particular, it might be well worth doing, because I am told, by people who ought to know, that runner bean seed is going to be scarce and expensive next year. Mind you, there is nothing official about this, I was told the same last year, but there seemed to be plenty about, but I believe we got some good supplies in from Eastern Europe last year, and we shan't get them this year. However, I'm not going to prophesy about seeds, our seed trade will see us through if it's humanly possible—they have never let us down yet; they seem to produce seeds under the most adverse and apparently impossible conditions, like conjurers fetching things out of a hat, but they manage it somehow, and so they will next year! And I shall get the usual crop of letters accusing the seedsmen of double dealing and profiteering, but anyone who knows anything of the seed trade will know better than that. In my opinion they are doing a grand job of work under the most difficult conditions. But where had I got to? Oh, yes, beans! I should think it must have been almost a record season for runner beans; they dropped off a lot without setting in the early part of the summer, probably due to the weather. Even I picked scores of perfect, straight beans, many of them fifteen and sixteen inches long, except during the week of our local show, when they wouldn't budge beyond a foot, and all turned their tails up. They straightened out after the show and grew longer than ever, and we have never been short of beans since.

Now what about that garden frame? I daresay you have had a cucumber or something in it for the summer, but that is about finished now and there is no need for the frame to remain idle. You could sow a few early cauliflowers in it for one thing, let them remain there for the winter and plant them out in the spring. We did that last year, and cut some very nice heads in June, before the peas and other good things arrived, and they were very welcome then. There is usually a waiting period in late June when there is very little to be had except spring cabbage, and these early cauliflowers make a pleasant change. There are several good early varieties to choose from— "All the year round" is a nice one, but there are others just as good. Or you might like to try growing mushrooms in a frame—it's a bit of a gamble, but not so difficult as some people try to make out. All you want is a couple of barrow loads of fresh stable manure, complete with straw; mix this with an equal amount of dead leaves from the trees, and turn it over a few times till it loses most of its steamy heat. Then empty the frame as deeply as you can, put the manure in and tread it down firmly, leave it for a couple of days and then get a packet of sterilized mushroom spawn. Press little bits of it, about the size of walnuts, into the manure, about a foot apart, and cover it over with about four inches of soil—old potting soil with plenty of sand and rotten leaf mould in it is excellent. Don't water it unless it is very dry, and if you do, do so before you put the spawn in, and let it evaporate the moisture before covering up. Finally, cover the whole frame over with old sacks or straw litter, and forget all about it for a month or two. Perhaps towards Christmas you will have a peep inside and find some nice little mushrooms. If you don't you won't have lost much, and the material will be good for the garden. I have had quite nice crops like this, but I remember one year I didn't get a sign of a mushroom, so in the late winter I cleared the whole lot out and dug it into the garden where the celery trench was to be. In due course, during the summer, the trench was dug and the celery planted, and lo and behold, mushrooms began to appear all along it, and we gathered quite a good crop. Mushrooms are strange things, they don't always obey orders, even those of the experts, but they are very interesting.

Another thing you can do with a corner of the cold frame is to sow sweet peas. My Henry objects to this! He says you can't eat sweet peas, so what's the good of growing them? Perhaps I ought to feel like that too, but I don't. I like sweet peas, and they don't occupy much room, so I see no reason why we shouldn't have a few. Anyway, we will compromise to satisfy Henry, and sow a few early green peas too. You can sow either green peas or sweet peas now in boxes, or in little pots; one seed in a pot, two in the case of green peas round seeded. We used to sow them in ice-cream cartons and egg shells, but these seem to be things of the past, and the future; whatever you put them in, by sowing them now, you can get them much earlier next year than by sowing them in the spring. They have to stop in the frame all the winter with just a little protection during very wet or severe weather, otherwise they need none at all. They won't grow much, but in the spring they will have plenty of roots and when you plant them out in March away they go. If you sow them in boxes put them in a good inch apart or they will get over-crowded. While on the subject of flowers, I should like just to mention hydrangeas, because so many people write to me about growing them. It is really quite a simple matter. At the present time a healthy hydrangea probably has a number of dead or dying flower heads on it, and also a number of young green shoots which have not flowered; these are the shoots which, with ordinary luck, will bear the flowers next year, so they must not be cut at all unless there are too many of them and you want to thin the weak ones out. But those shoots which have flowered and still have the dead flowers on them should be cut back—not merely the flower head, but a good length of the stem with it, leaving only two pairs of leaves at the bottom; from these new shoots will appear in the spring for flowering later on. In the kitchen garden there is always the question of manure shortage cropping up, especially bulky manures to supply humus, which are almost unobtainable in urban districts, so it's no use moaning about it, we must find a substitute. Of course you've got the compost heap for digging in later on which is a great help, but there is still another way of supplying humus, by means of growing a green crop and digging it back into the ground in the spring. For sowing now you must have something which will stand through the winter; mustard wouldn't do—the hard weather would kill it, it is excellent for spring sowing but not now. Vetches or rye, or a mixture of both, are quite good, if obtainable, but I think turnips are even better, because they serve a double purpose. Green top stone is a suitable variety, and there are others in the catalogues marked for autumn sowing. If you have patches of vacant ground not wanted till the spring, sow these turnips on them, rather thinly, either broadcast or in rows a foot apart, to allow for hoeing. They will grow a bit before the winter, more or less according to weather, then stand still till early spring, when they will blossom forth into tender greenery. You can gather a few boilings of first turnip tops, and then dig the remainder back into the soil where they will serve a useful purpose as manure.

October

FRUITY SUBJECTS

I WAS in an orchard the other day where nearly every apple tree had quite a heavy crop. It made me quite envious when I thought of my own measly lot, which won't fill a bushel basket altogether, but it was also comforting to know that Jack Frost left some districts alone, and I hope those of you who are lucky enough to have a crop will take great care of them, especially the late varieties which can be kept till the spring, for if I'm anything of a prophet there won't be too many apples about then. The first essential is to gather them at the right time and in good condition. There are several ways of gathering apples; you can shake them off, or knock them with the clothes prop, or throw sticks at them, and I must confess I have still enough of the schoolboy in me rather to enjoy this method, especially if they happen to be somebody else's apples, but I'm afraid such methods won't do at all if you want to keep them. You cannot be too careful in handling apples—they should never be tugged or twisted off, it is much better to leave them on the tree till they come off easily, and you should be very careful not to bruise them in any way; tipping them out of a basket or anything like that quite often makes a little bruise which starts decay, and it is the easiest thing in the world to stick your thumb nail into them and spoil them that way. So handle them very carefully, good keeping apples are none too plentiful these days. The next thing is to choose the most suitable place to keep them. What are the ideal conditions for a fruit room? Easier said than done, I'm afraid, but it is always as well to have an ideal to aim at, and get as near to it as circumstances will allow. The perfect fruit room is a low building with a thatched roof, a floor of natural earth, and a little ventilation, but not too much. The thatched roof maintains an even temperature, and is very effective against frost. Apples like to be kept cool, very cool, so long as they do not get frozen—ordinary living rooms are usually warm by day and cold at night, and are not suitable. They are also too dry—if apples are kept in a dry place they soon begin to shrivel, especially if it is warm as well; a loft, for instance, with a wooden floor, is usually too dry to keep the quality and flavour in apples, that is why an earth floor is an advantage; it allows a certain amount of moisture to rise and prevent the atmosphere getting too dry.

The fruit-storing trays, which are sold for the purpose, are excellent, provided they are in the right sort of building, but not if you put them in the back kitchen near the copper fire, as I saw someone doing recently. An old shed or disused stable is quite a good place, and I, personally, would rather put apples on bare boards or shelves than on straw, because straw has a tendency to impart a peculiar flavour to them—so does old newspaper. The specially made oiled apple papers are excellent if you can get them, or have a supply in hand; you can wrap each apple separately in one of these and they keep perfectly, but I don't know what the supply is like at the moment. I once kept apples in perfect condition till May by what I should think must be the simplest method of all. I collected together all the old wooden boxes I could find, of various shapes and sizes, filled them with apples, one apple at a time, not tipping them out of the basket. I put them in the boxes just as they were, without paper or anything else, and then stacked the boxes out of doors against a wall, covered them up well with old sacks, bundles of fish netting, and all sorts of odds and ends of that kind, and finally put a few pieces of corrugated iron over the lot to keep the wet out. We had some pretty sharp frosts while they were there, and the whole pile was buried under snow for a time, but the apples were well protected. We took out a box at a time as required, and there were very few bad ones among them. You can, of course, store them in clamps, like potatoes. I have seen Bramley Seedling taken out of clamps in March as fresh and green as when they were put in. Commercial growers put them into cold storage, or even gas chambers, but I'm afraid that sort of thing is beyond most of us, so we have to do the best we can with what we have. Cold storage, in this case, doesn't mean freezing—apples wouldn't stand that—they are kept a few degrees above freezing-point, without varying, and they fetch them out again in the spring in perfect condition. So avoid warm rooms above all other things. One other thing; be careful about rats—if there are any about the premises they are pretty sure to find them, and nibble holes in them. So, if necessary, you must protect them with wire netting or something.

Pears are rather different to apples; you can keep them until they are ripe, but not after that. A pear never seems to stand still, the process of ripening merges into that of decay, so that once it is ripe it soon begins to go bad in the middle, and so far as I know there is no way of preventing it; so it is best to keep pears on a shelf or in trays where they can be watched, and as soon as they are ripe that is the time to eat them. Most pears are at their best only for a few days, and if you don't eat them then you probably won't eat them at all. So much for storing, but while we are on the subject, I may as well mention quinces, not the ordinary yellow quince, but the Japanese quince, Cydonia Japonica, commonly called Japonica, and grown on the walls of houses, not for its fruit but for its pretty pink and red flowers in the spring. Every year listeners send me the fruits of this plant—greenish, hard things that you could play cricket with, and ask me if I have ever seen them before, and whether they are of any use. You don't usually get many of them, but if you do the best thing to do is to make jelly with them; they make a lovely orange-coloured jelly with a very distinctive flavour. They also add a pleasant flavour to an apple pudding—just one, chopped up or grated very finely, and mixed with the apples. If you put it in whole, or merely cut up in chunks, they would still be hard after the apples were cooked. There is one variety of these quinces, or Cydonias, called cydonia mauleii, which has pretty orange-coloured flowers in the spring, and smallish golden-yellow fruits in the autumn. These fruits are strongly and pleasantly scented, and half a dozen in a bowl in a warm room give off a very nice perfume, and last up till Christmas or longer.

But I suppose we had better concern ourselves more, for the time being, with the useful fruits which we can eat. So what about choosing a few good apples for planting this autumn? Good trees are none too plentiful, and it will be a case of the early bird catching the best of them, so although you may not plant till November, it would be wise to order them well in advance just to make sure, and always remember that it is just as easy to plant a good variety of apple or pear, which will give you pleasure and satisfaction, as it is to plant a second-rater—so the first thing to do is to choose carefully. Many of my friends seem to be in a hurry; they want to plant a tree this year and gather a nice crop of apples from it next year. I'm afraid that can't be done, but it is possible to gather good fruit in the second year if you plant the right type of tree. I daresay you have heard a good deal about the different crab stocks which apple trees are budded or grafted on. These range from very dwarf kinds, which make only small trees not much bigger than black currant bushes, to strong tall growers which make the big orchard tree, and they transmit their particular habit of growth to the tree which

2*

is grafted on them. So if you like, by choosing the right types of stock, you could have two trees of Cox's Orange Pippin apple, one a dwarf bush, and the other a tall tree. The dwarf crab stocks are usually spoken of as "Paradise" stocks, but the word means little or nothing—it was merely the name of a field where the stocks were planted when they first came over from the Continent, and there were several varieties of them. These have since been sorted out and classified under numbers. I'm not going to confuse you with a lengthy description of them, but the dwarfest of them all is now known as type 9. Apples budded or grafted on this stock are like Peter Pan—they don't grow up, they remain dwarf and bushy. They also start bearing fruit very quickly, so it is possible to plant these little trees about the garden, about six feet apart, and gather fruit from them while the larger types of trees are growing up. I saw some this year, planted two years ago, none of them more than 4 or 5 feet high, but each bearing 30 to 40 perfect apples. So if you want quick returns, try to get trees on type 9 stock. I say "try" because, although there are some about in the best fruit nurseries, the stock is limited. I only recommend these type 9 stocks as novelty small trees to fruit quickly. There is much to be said against them. Some of the other stocks are better, and if you want trees to grow up and last a bit longer, try to get them on the number 2 stock, which many nurserymen use, and is the most suitable for trained trees such as cordons. For bigger trees, it is better to leave it to the nurseryman. Having decided on the type of trees, the next thing is to choose the varieties, and the question as to which is the best dessert apple is an impossible one to answer; it depends on which you like best, but it also depends on other things—district, soil, and so on. It is no use planting an ultra choice variety which won't grow. I suppose 90 out of 100 would vote for Cox's Orange Pippin as the finest dessert apple; so would I, but I wouldn't plant it, because I know it to be a delicate, exacting variety, and it wouldn't succeed on the heavy, cold soil of my district, so it is better to choose one that will. Actually, I consider that there are new varieties of apples to be had now which in many respects are superior to the much-boosted Cox's. I notice that the Food Controller has named three apples to be classed together as the luxury apples, to be controlled at the highest price; these are Cox's Orange Pippin, Laxton's Superb, and Ellison's Orange. There are others equally good, but not yet grown in sufficient quantities for market to warrant their inclusion. Of the three I should choose Superb as the finest of all Christmas apples—a heavy cropper, good keeper, delicious flavour, and succeeds on almost any soil, even on heavy clay. A safe speculation for any garden. Ellison's Orange, the other of the chosen three, is an earlier apple, being eaten now. It has a distinct flavour, almost suggestive of aniseed, but very pleasant aniseed, and it also bears an excellent character as a garden apple. Of the more modern varieties there are three or four bearing the name of Laxton, the raiser of them, which are worthy of a place in every garden. The earliest one is Laxton's Advance, a pretty apple of delicious flavour, ready in August. This is followed by one called Epicure, which to my mind is easily the best of all the September apples. The next is Lord Lambourne, one of the most reliable croppers of all, and a lovely apple, too, ready in October. Another which lasts till Christmas is Laxton's Fortune, which, when it gets better known, will probably be quite as popular as Cox's Pippin; its flavour is delicious, there is no other word for it. Follow this with Superb, which I have already mentioned, and you have as good a set of dessert apples as anyone need wish for. You should be able to get all these from any good fruit nursery—there are no patents or copyrights in fruit trees.

39

Of cooking apples for the ordinary garden I shall recommend only three: Early Victoria to start with, which is one of the yellowy-green Codlin types ready before summer is over; Monarch, an excellent autumn apple, rather brightly coloured for a cooker, but sweeter than most of them, and therefore needs less sugar—a very reliable cropper too. The last is King Edward VII, a round, green apple which crops well and keeps till apples come again. I haven't forgotten Bramley Seedling, one of the best of the late-keeping cooking apples, but it makes a big strong tree, and where space is limited I consider King Edward VII more suitable; in quality it is about equal to Bramley Seedling, but its growth is less vigorous

FRUIT AND VEGETABLES

A fortnight ago I was talking about storing apples. This has brought an interesting letter from a commercial fruit grower about the controlled prices of apples. He points out that prices to the growers have been fixed, remaining the same throughout the season. Thus, presumably, the price to the grower for, say Bramley Seedling or other good-keeping apples, will be the same after Christmas as it is now. The result of this, and I am quoting the grower, is that it won't pay them to store apples to spread them over the season as they do in normal times, but they will be more likely to market them all as quickly as possible and have done with them. This may lead to plentiful supplies between now and Christmas, but precious little after that. I daresay there are good reasons for this method of fixing prices, at any rate, it is not for me to question it, but what I am going to suggest is that we do as much spreading over ourselves as we possibly can. It seems a pity to use up such good keepers as Bramley Seedlings, Lane's Prince Albert, and other late varieties before the earlier kinds are finished, so I suggest that if you have any good keepers put them into store for use later on, and buy apples from the shops as long as the supply is good and plentiful. If you haven't any of your own it might be good policy to buy a bushel or two of good keepers and put them away, otherwise, if we don't make provision for ourselves, apples may be non-existent before the winter is over.

What a lot of maggoty apples there are this year! Every post for a month or so has brought me samples of either the apples or the maggots, or S.O.S. letters about them, but I'm afraid nothing can be done about it now; you can't very well get the maggots out of the apples, or repair the damage they have left behind. I'm afraid a good many gardeners are rather like the Foolish Virgins, they do not look ahead and insure against these pests and troubles. Let us take a lesson from some of these minor disasters and try to prevent them next year—it's no use waiting till they are with us and then getting panicky! Take these maggoty apples, for instance; as far as I have been able to observe, it is mainly the work of the apple sawfly, although the Codlin moth has also had a hand in the game. The sawfly is just an ordinary looking fly and like other flies it has a nasty habit of laying eggs where nobody wants them—in this particular case, on the tiny apples just as they are beginning to develop. These eggs very soon hatch, and the baby maggots, being hungry, begin to eat the little apples, and to get away from the tom-tits and other birds who are on the lookout for them, and to protect themselves from the weather, they bore a little tunnel into the apple and get inside it. You know the rest of the story. The Codlin moth is the other culprit, and its effect on the apple is very similar; it lays an egg in the open flower, or the eye of a tiny apple, the young caterpillar tunnels down to the core, eats the pips and centre, and then tunnels out through the side. Do these habits suggest a remedy to you? It is obvious that the only time we can stop this little game is at the egg-laying season by spraying the trees with derris insecticide as soon as the blossoms have fallen and the bees are no longer at work on them, and repeating it about twice at ten day intervals. This makes it very difficult for the flies and moths to lay their eggs in comfort and also destroys the newly-hatched maggots. You will probably hear more about this in the proper season, but perhaps you would like to make a note in your diary about it while the subject is rather prominent. There is one apple tree pest which you can deal with now, or very soon, and that is the woolly aphis, or American blight, which looks like white cotton-wool on the trees. I have seen trees lately with all the young stems, as well as the old branches, simply covered with it. If you remove this woolly covering you will find clusters of small reddish insects which suck the sap out of trees and do them a great deal of harm. Unfortunately, ordinary sprays like nicotine and derris do not penetrate the greasy woolly substance, so a few years ago I chanced my arm on something a bit stronger—the well-known tar-oil winter wash diluted to one in twelve. This was quite an unorthodox method of dealing with woolly aphis, and I don't think you will find it in any official publications, but I was prepared to take risks with a particularly lousy tree. Tar-oil wash is, of course, essentially a dormant season wash, it easily injures growing plants and green leaves and shoots, so you can't use it where fresh green vegetables or other plants are growing. But there was nothing to hurt near my tree, so I waited till the apples were all gathered and then I let fly, and gave the tree a good hard spraying from top to bottom, a sort of kill or cure remedy. The leaves soon came off, but they were coming off anyway, so that didn't matter much, and the woolly aphis came off too, and the tree has been clean ever since and suffered no harm. I have given others the same medicine since, usually fairly late in October, and with good results. I pass on the idea for what it is worth, but don't forget that tar-oil winter wash destroys green leaves and growing plants, so be careful how you use it. I am only suggesting it now for bad cases of woolly aphis.

Another trouble which has been very prevalent this year, if my post-bag is anything to go by, is blight on outdoor tomatoes. I must have received a bushel of rotten tomatoes lately, and I haven't felt a bit grateful for them—neither has our postman! You ought to see them, and smell them, sometimes; but I suppose it's all in the day's work! The unfortunate thing is that nothing can be done about it when it is on the fruit; it is the same disease or blight which attacks the potatoes, and it can be prevented by spraying the plants in the summer with Bordeaux or Burgundy mixture when the potatoes are sprayed. I don't like saying I told you so, or that you were duly warned, but do let us try to remember these things at the proper season in future. We could reduce our losses very considerably if we would only take timely measures, and it is so much easier.

Now let us turn to the vegetable plots and see how the crops are looking. Not much to complain about as far as the root crops are concerned, and the winter greens are not looking at all bad, except that here and there I notice that caterpillars are beginning to get busy, and I have also seen a few white flies on the brussels sprouts. Nothing serious so far perhaps, but how quickly these troubles can spread if we don't tackle them. Get in a stock of derris powder and blow it about through the plants, or mix up a wet derris insecticide and spray them with it, or even pour it over them with a water can with a fine rose on. It won't take long and it may save them from disaster, and so long as you are not eating them for a week or two it will do no harm.

One of the main jobs now is to plant out the spring cabbages. The ground should be ready for them, and it doesn't need much getting ready for this job. If you were planting in the spring you would dig and manure the ground, because, with the improving weather, the plants are encouraged to make rapid growth without any checks, but in the autumn it is different; to encourage soft young growth now, especially if we get a mild autumn, means that the plants may be too tender to survive the winter, so I suggest that you merely clean the ground, sprinkle lime over it at the rate of half a pound to the square yard, lightly fork over the surface, and plant the cabbages with a trowel as firmly as possible; they will then settle themselves down comfortably and make slow but healthy growth, and the winter won't hurt them. When you take young cabbage plants from the seed bed, don't just pull them out, as some people do, and leave half the roots behind; it is true they usually recover, but there is no reason why they should be subjected to such cruelty. If the soil is dry, give them a soaking first, and then put a fork under to loosen them, so that they come out without injuring the roots; they get on much better after that, and it doesn't take much longer, and, if necessary, water them after planting, to settle the soil round the roots. The usual distance for planting cabbages is eighteen inches apart, and, of course, they need that amount of space to do themselves justice, but I usually plant them nine inches apart, with eighteen inches between the rows. It may be my fancy, but they seem more comfortable closer together and settle down for the winter better. But the real reason is that when they begin to grow in the spring and touch each other you can pull out every other one; that is usually in late March, when green stuff is getting scarce. The

44

others, of course, you leave to heart up into proper cabbages. Two years ago a friend of mine who does a bit of selling planted them like this, and he made more money out of the half-grown ones, sold as early greens, than he did out of the later cabbages. It doesn't always happen like that, but it is worth doing as a rule; young plants are usually fairly plentiful at this time of the year. I shouldn't delay any longer if I were you. I know that some people will still be planting cabbages in November, but they won't have such a good chance to settle down for the winter, especially if we get a cold autumn.

The treatment for winter or spring lettuces, which should also be planted out now, is about the same as that for cabbages, except that they don't need the lime, and they don't need so much room—a foot apart is usually enough, or even a little bit closer. Lettuces are not quite so hardy as cabbages, so it is advisable to give them a position near a wall or building if you can, which shelters them from the north and east.

A crop which can be sown now with a good chance of getting early results is the broad bean. The great value of broad beans lies in their earliness, they are not much appreciated later in the summer when the peas are about, but by sowing them now you can often get them much earlier, and cleaner too, and they will stand through all but the hardest of winters, especially the Longpod varieties. What they don't like is a very wet winter, or soil which gets waterlogged, so you must choose a well-drained site for them. The way I do it is to fork over the soil and get a nice fine surface with the rake, then, instead of making drills, press the seeds into the soil and afterwards draw a little more soil over them with the hoe. The best plan, I think, is to put them in a double row, with the beans six inches apart each way, then a space of eighteen inches and another double row.

45

If you have an asparagus bed it will need a little attention now or very soon. First cut off carefully all the stems which are bearing berries; this is best done before they are ripe, to prevent the berries dropping on the bed and producing a crowd of seedlings. Then, as soon as the foliage has turned yellow, cut it all down at ground level, and burn it—it is no use on the compost heap. Then pull out all the weeds and clean up the bed, fork it over lightly, and spread a layer of old manure or hop manure over it, covering this in turn with soil taken from along the sides of the bed. This prevents the birds scratching the manure about and also makes a good drainage channel to take away the surplus water, for the one thing asparagus doesn't like is to have its toes in cold water all the winter.

AUTUMN REMINDERS

Life, they say, is full of troubles—so are potatoes! What with blight and scab and slugs and wireworms, it's a wonder we are able to grow them at all, yet, in spite of all their troubles, I have seen some of the finest crops ever being lifted lately. Now I want to mention another potato enemy which may be new to many of you, and that is the potato eelworm. Sorry to talk about it in the middle of Sunday dinner, but it's the only chance I get, and it won't take more than a minute or two. Earlier in the season, when potatoes were being lifted, some of my friends pointed out tiny white specks on the tubers, and others wrote to me about them. These little specks were most likely caused by this eelworm and they were probably clusters of its eggs. This eelworm is a microscopic creature, much too small to be seen with the naked eye, but it gets into the stems and roots of plants in large numbers and cripples the plants, making them look very sick and sorry without any apparent reason for it; it has often been

46

thought to be a disease of some sort. A good many kinds of plants are attacked by eelworms, they are very common in certain flowering plants, particularly phloxes. You have probably seen those plants twisted and crippled by them. Fortunately, they are rather like the aphis family, there are different varieties of them, and they stick more or less to one type of plant; thus the phlox eelworm does not attack the potato, and the potato eelworm sticks more or less to potatoes or allied plants, such as tomatoes. Once they are there it is very difficult to do anything about it. Those little white specks on the potatoes, which contain the eggs, usually drop off or get rubbed off, when the potatoes are mature, and are left in the soil ready to attack the next crop, and, of course, if they can go on increasing and multiplying, they will soon make it impossible to grow potatoes on that particular ground, so what I want to suggest is that in making your plans for next year, you should choose a different place for the potato crop, as far away from this year's crop as possible. Eelworm makes a good system of rotation more important than ever. So far you may not have been troubled, it is not prevalent everywhere, but it has been pretty bad this year in parts of Yorkshire and the North, and if these things are neglected they have a way of spreading rather rapidly, so let us bear it in mind and not plant potatoes on the same ground in successive years, or we may be asking for serious trouble.

Mine are all lifted and in store now, mostly Arran Banner and Majestic, and the only fault I have to find with them, if it is a fault, is that there are too many big ones—great coarse things weighing a pound or more. We shan't be short of baking potatoes this time, and it seems the same all over my district, last year we could not get enough bakers. I like baked potatoes, but I've got a special way of preparing them. Would you like me to give you a recipe for a winter supper? I don't want to steal any of Freddie

47

Grisewood's Kitchen Front thunder, but we'll chance it for once. Here it is:—

First bake several large potatoes in the usual way and when they are done cut the top end off or, if they are big long ones, you can cut them in half. Then scoop out all the insides and put it in a basin. Add milk, pepper and salt, a little butter or marg., a couple of eggs, if you feel extravagant, and any sort of seasoning or flavouring which may appeal to you, grated cheese, tomato sauce, chopped onions, bits of chopped bacon or liver left over from breakfast; that's the beauty of this recipe, you can put anything you like in it according to taste—not all these things together, mind, but just what you happen to fancy to make a nice savoury concoction. Then you mix it up well in the basin till it is about the consistency of thick clotted cream, put it back into the potato jackets, stand them in a baking tin in the oven for about 20 minutes, and then sit round the fire and eat them with a spoon. The best way is to put them into tea-cups and eat them like boiled eggs in an egg-cup. Just you try it once or twice till you get the right flavour and consistency, and let me know what you think of it. I suppose really I ought to have sold the idea to Lord Woolton, but I'm in generous mood to-day so I'm letting you have it for nothing.

Very well, I seem to have got away with that, so now back to gardening and a word about shallots. Early this year shallot bulbs were very difficult to get, so a good many people grew them from seed and got quite respectable crops that way. It is quite a new idea to some gardeners to grow shallots from a packet of seed and they have been pleasantly surprised by the results. But there is a snag in it. These shallot bulbs which have been grown from seed are no use for planting in the spring; you won't get a crop of shallots from them if you do, they will simply run up to seed. As a matter of fact, they are not true shallots at all, but a type of onion which resembles the shallot. So if you like them and want some more, get another packet of seed in the spring and repeat the performance, but if you prefer to plant bulbs, make sure that you get the true shallot.

I am sorry to find that even now there is still far too much waste going on in gardens and allotments. I have lately come across heaps of small and damaged potatoes, crooked, split carrots and other roots, old loose green cauliflowers, and all sorts of similar things thrown together on the rubbish heap. Admittedly, these things may not be good enough for the kitchen, but what about the pigs and poultry? I daresay the average allotment holder or suburban gardener has no direct interest in either pigs or chickens, but those who keep them are having the dickens of a job to find food enough for them, so it is a pity if we can't think of a scheme for using the good stuff which is available. I should think where municipal pig centres exist they might very well include allotments in their collecting schemes—perhaps they do in many districts—I hope so.

I spoke to one typical allotment holder who had a couple of barrow loads of waste potatoes and roots, and old damaged marrows, and he said anybody could have them if they liked to fetch them, but he couldn't afford the time to run about with them, and I quite appreciate this point of view. If I had kept a pig myself I should certainly get in touch with the allotment holders just now and collect a few barrow loads of good stuff for boiling up. Many vegetable plots just now are covered with weeds, and the question arises as to whether they should be cleared up and destroyed, or dug into the ground as manure. It all depends on what they are. Perennial weeds, such as dandelions and couch grass, or those with big thick roots are best out of it and on the bonfire; if you dig them in you will merely be transplanting them. On the other hand, annual weeds like chickweed and groundsel, as well as all the waste vegetable leaves, can either be put on the compost heap or dug in now as and where they are. I always dig them in green and start a new compost heap in the spring; I don't have one during the winter after the old one has been used up. I should if I had a lot of autumn leaves to collect from the trees, but I haven't. I often pick up useful tips from old countrymen. I watched one the other day digging up his main crop potatoes; as he lifted the crop he dug and manured the ground all in one operation. He started across one end of the plot digging the potatoes and keeping a good open trench. During the summer he has been stacking pig muck at the end of the plot, and his schoolboy son or grandson was spreading this along the trench as he dug, while another picked up the potatoes and collected the haulms into a heap. He was throwing the soil up rough and he won't need to touch it again till the spring. I envy him. My potato ground still has the old haulms and rubbish scattered about it waiting to be cleared up, and then it will have to be dug, perhaps when the weather isn't nearly so nice. We live and learn.

Now what about those little front gardens in urban districts? I mean, they are not growing much in the way of food crops, and I am not suggesting that they should. I consider the back garden is the place for the vegetable crops rather than the small front one, although, I must admit, I have seen a few interesting examples of what can be done in war time even with a little front garden; tomatoes all round the bay window and an attractive scheme with beetroots and carrots and such like. But whether it's flowers or vegetables, I am all for keeping the front tidy and smart as far as is possible, and even if you have had food crops there in the summer, there is nothing much you can do now until the spring comes round again, so why not a nice show of spring flowers? They can cheer us up wonderfully after a dark long winter, and they can all be out of the way in time to plant tomatoes again next year. I find, even if you haven't grown any, it is fairly easy to pick up a few nice flowering plants for putting out now—wallflowers, for instance. You always feel that the winter is over when you see and smell a nice border or bed of wallflowers, and there are some lovely colours in them now. Most of the local nurseries have got a few for sale, so have a look round and see what you can find. Wallflowers do well in most gardens and they keep the garden furnished with a little greenery even in the winter. Give them a little lime before planting, and plant them firmly; that's all they ask for. They belong to the same botanical order as the cabbages and get club root, and a little lime often keeps it in check. A border of scarlet, blood-red and yellow wallflowers, or a mixture of all the colours you can get, with blue forget-me-nots in front of them, take a bit of beating for a spring display. Unfortunately, bulbs this year are scarce, beyond a limited number of home-grown tulips and daffodils and a few odds and ends. If you can get them a few May flowering tulips among the wallflowers add to the colour scheme. You might be able to pick up a few of the smaller bulbs if you know a friend who has them. I am planting a few snowdrops and crocuses dug out of an old neglected garden. I happened to know just where to look for them. I am very fond of snowdrops, and I find the best way to plant them if you have to dig them up first, is to dig up a complete spit of soil with the spade with the snowdrop bulbs in it, and drop it into a hole prepared for it. And you have to dig pretty deep for them too. Snowdrop bulbs which have been there a long time are often a spade's depth below the surface. Crocuses, too, seem to get deeper when they are left to themselves. Double daisies make a good show in the spring; I had some of the big pink and white ones, and also some of the little ones like pink buttons, called Dresden china. I borrowed a good clump of them, and divided them up into separate little plants, and put them about three inches apart; they start flowering very early in the spring and last for a long time. The so-called winter flowering pansies which were sown in July can be transplanted now. It is true you occasionally see odd flowers on them during the winter, but they usually put up their best show in March, and you get some fine flowers then. Another lovely little spring flower is the purple primrose, Wanda; it flowers very freely and starts as early as February. Any of the coloured primroses are nice, and there are quite a lot of them about now, and they do quite well even in shady corners. Polyanthuses, too, make a grand spring show. I saved some of the brightest coloured ones from a blitzed garden last spring, and planted them in an odd corner, so I shan't have to buy or scrounge any now! Pinks, too, are delightful flowers in any garden, and if you pick up a few old roots, tear them to pieces and plant them now, they will settle down quite well and flower in the spring. If it's only a front border a few yards long or a few odd corners beside the path, a little time and trouble spent now with mixed spring flowers will be well rewarded when the winter is over.

November

PLANTING NEW FRUIT TREES

A WEEK or two ago I was suggesting a few good varieties of
dessert apples for planting in the small garden. Since then
I have been asked to recommend a few good cooking
varieties. It isn't easy; no one could pick out, say six
apples, and say they were the best—it depends on so many
things, your local soil and circumstances, personal tastes,
and so on, and the best I or anyone can do is to suggest
those which experience teaches us are the most suitable
under general conditions. We all have our favourites, and,
I like to make this clear, I am only giving you my personal
opinions, someone else might suggest half a dozen apples,
all different to mine, but quite as good, or even better in
his garden. The apple which seems most in demand is a
good late-keeping cooker for use in the late winter and
early spring, and I suppose nine out of ten experts would
put Bramley Seedling at the top of the list. So should I for
a large garden or orchard. It's a grand apple, good quality,
good cropper, and keeps perfectly, but I shouldn't recommend it for a small garden. That sounds rather contradictory, and reminds me of the old countryman who was
discussing his late lamented wife. "Ah, Minister," he said,
"she was a wonderful wife, nothing too much trouble for
her. For forty years she allus had a good meal and a cheery
smile ready for me; kind and loving, never said a cross
word; a perfect wife if ever there was one, Minister, but
somehow I never liked the woman!"

My only objection to Bramley Seedling for a small
garden is that it grows too strongly and makes too large a
tree and soon gets in the way, and its growth is so vigorous
that it doesn't lend itself well to training or restricted
growth. Where there is plenty of room to let it grow freely,

53

then Bramley Seedling by all means, but where space is restricted I would rather have King Edward VII. This is a hard green apple, very similar in quality to Bramley Seedling and keeps just as well, but it is more suitable for the smaller type of garden tree. I have kept King Edward VII till June without any special treatment, and it seems to produce healthy crops on nearly all types of soil, and even in the North. Lane's Prince Albert is another good reliable cooker, an oldish apple but still one of the best and keeps well. Another not perhaps so well known is Monarch, a coloured, rather handsome apple. Most people seem to like a green apple for cooking. I don't know why. Monarch is an excellent cooker, rather sweeter than most and therefore requires less sugar; it is also a good cropper and keeper. The best, in my opinion, of the early cookers for using straight from the tree in late summer, is Early Victoria, a yellow Codlin type of apple which is very reliable. Perhaps the best of the autumn cookers is a more modern one called Arthur Turner, a fine big apple and a good cropper, well worth planting on the lawn for the sake of its wonderful deep pink blossom, which is exceptionally fine. I'm afraid that will have to do. I could go on talking about apples for a long time, there are so many interesting varieties that the subject is almost inexhaustible, but there is a clock in this studio and you can see it moving. So what about one or two pear trees? There are some lovely pears in existence, and also some unlovely ones, and you need to be more careful in choosing pears than apples, because some of the best of them are rather exacting in their requirements. In an ordinary garden it is perhaps better to consider cropping powers and reliability rather than super quality, or to aim at a combination of both. There are some very nice new pears about now, but I don't know enough about them yet to recommend them. The one pear which, to my mind, combines all the good points is Conference, and if I had only room for one I shouldn't hesitate about it. Conference is a healthy grower, self-fertile, good and regular cropper and of first-class quality, usually ready in late October. The worst of pears is that if you have a heavy crop of one sort you have to eat them all up within a week or two while they are at their best. I have only one good tree of Conference, but we nearly always have to give a lot away to prevent them going bad, so if you want a long season of pears it is best to have one tree each of three or four varieties carefully selected to follow each other in ripening. There's another advantage in this, many varieties are self-sterile and need others to cross-pollinate them. Conference is an exception. Professional gardeners don't need my advice on this, so for the amateur back gardener I would suggest three or four varieties which may not be quite so finely flavoured as, say, the aristocratic Doyenne du Comice, but are more likely to give you a crop of good pears. For an early one, Dr. Jules Guyot; this is very much like the well-known "William" pear, but a better cropper. "Fertility" is a good September pear, rather small and not of the highest quality, but very reliable and acceptable. Conference, already mentioned, follows this, then I would suggest Marie Louise, one of those big, fine melting pears. If you want to grow one on a wall or in a sunny corner, plant Doyenne du Comice, the finest pear of all when you get it, but it needs others near it to cross-pollinate it, it's no use planting it alone.

I don't know whether it is worth while planting plums in these days, especially cooking plums, but I think there is something very nice about a good ripe plum, so we ought to have a tree or two if we can find room for them. If you like an early plum in the summer, and most of us do, there is a fairly new one called Early Laxton. I gathered some fully ripe on August Bank Holiday; it is red and yellow, something like a little Victoria to look at, and very juicy and sweet. Victoria is a grand old plum, still one of the best to plant in spite of its susceptibility to silver leaf disease. And if you like a late plum plant a tree of Coe's Golden Crop, a big egg-shaped yellow one, and to my mind the finest flavoured dessert plum of the lot. It gets ripe in October when nearly all the others are over, and the longer it hangs on the tree the sweeter it gets. But it's no use planting it alone, it needs others to cross-pollinate it. This is, of course, the chief difficulty in some cases, especially in a small back garden. Suppose, for instance, you had only room for one apple, one pear, and one plum. Which would you choose? If you went by super quality they would probably be Cox's Orange Pippin apple, Doyenne du Comice pear, and Jefferson Gage plum, but they are all self-sterile and you might never get a fruit on them. So I should suggest Laxton's Superb apple, Conference pear, and Victoria plum. They are all self-fertile and would fruit freely without any other varieties near them. It is a point worth bearing in mind when making a choice.

Now what about the bush fruits? While we are on the job we may as well choose a few. Of the raspberries I should put Red Cross and Norfolk Giant as the two best. The variety, Lloyd George, has had a popular run, but it has many faults; for one thing it doesn't always stop in its row but throws up its best canes all over the place, and it soon begins to deteriorate. It has one good point; if you cut it right down to the ground in March it often produces a good crop of raspberries in the autumn when the others are over, but for my part I prefer raspberries in the summer, and Red Cross is my first choice.

Of the black currants there are several good ones to choose from, and a local gardener might put you on to the best for your own district, but if in any doubt about it plant Boskoop Giant, an old one, but still one of the finest black currants in existence; why not propagate a few yourselves? It's one of the easiest things in the world if you've got some good healthy bushes, or know somebody who has, to take cuttings from. It's a bit late now, but not too late if you lose no more time. A cutting consists of a length of a young shoot which has grown this year. You cut a piece about a foot long containing six eyes or buds, cut it off just below a bud at the bottom end and just above a bud at the top end. Plant it firmly upright, with the lower three buds under the ground and the top three above. Plant three cuttings together in a triangle, nine inches apart, and just leave them there, keep them free from weeds, and in a couple of years the three cuttings together will form a nice bush, and there you are.

Gooseberries are like the apples, too many of them to choose from. If you want them for picking green I would suggest Whinham's Industry, a red one, and Keepsake, a yellow one. If you like to eat them ripe for dessert, try Golden Drop, Greengage, and Leveller. Leveller is the great big greeny-yellow one you see in the fruit shops sold in punnets. Golden Drop and Greengage are small but delicious in flavour.

Now take my tip and buy your fruit trees from a reliable source. There are plenty of good fruit nurseries of long standing and high reputation. There are also people who will sell you any rubbish at a low price, which may bring you nothing but disappointment. People frequently complain to me about being swindled; things have not turned out to be what they were said to be, and so on, but it's no use complaining to me, I can't do anything about it. If a good nurseryman makes a mistake he will put it right, a bad one won't. Another thing is that good fruit trees are likely to be scarce, so order them early or the ones you want will all be gone.

Now just a word or two about planting. You can plant

fruit trees any time from now till March. November is always considered the best planting month, but it is much better to go by the condition of the soil than the date. Don't plant when the ground is wet and sticky, you do more harm than good. Wait till the soil is workable and you can tread about on it without getting plastered up with mud. If the new trees have arrived and the ground isn't fit for them, just dig a trench, put the roots in and cover them with soil and they will be quite happy for the time being. Drainage is an important factor in successful fruit growing; trees do not grow well in water-logged soil. So dig it deeply before planting, but don't put a lot of heavy manure in it, young trees don't need manure, especially newly-planted trees. Transplanting is a surgical operation, the young tree has usually lost its fine thread-like feeding roots, however carefully it has been lifted, and its first job is to recover from the operation and build up a new system of feeding roots. It will do this much better with its main roots in normal soil than in contact with strong manure which is like poison to them. Take a little trouble over planting; trees usually recover more or less if you squeeze the roots into a narrow hole and push them down with a spade, but they do so much better if you don't. Make a wide shallow hole with the soil raised up a little in the centre to form a slight mound. Rest the base of the tree on this and spread the roots out around it. Then cover them with soil, a little at a time, treading it down very firmly so that by the time you've finished the tree isn't easily pulled out. You needn't jump on the roots and bruise them with hobnailed boots, but firm planting is essential. And don't plant too deeply, this is the commonest fault of all. So long as a young tree is firmly anchored the shallower you plant it the better. If it needs a stake for support, and most trees do, put the stake in first, don't drive it through the roots and loosen them afterwards. Finish with a good watering to settle the soil round the roots, and in the spring if you can spread a little strawy manure over the soil to keep the roots cool and moist during their first. summer, all will be well. Perhaps if you were planting trees by the acre you wouldn't be able to go to all this trouble, but with a few odd ones in the garden you can, and it pays.

MAINLY SPADE WORK

I hope you are looking after the autumn vegetable crops, storing everything worth storing, and keeping the greens free of caterpillars, and so on. I had a look at my potatoes the other day, and although I thought they were in excellent condition when I lifted them, I find that a surprising number of them are showing signs of trouble; blight, I suppose. I shall have to sort them over carefully, and I would advise you to do the same if you can; if you get one or two rotten ones they soon spread the trouble to others. A little dry powdered lime dusted among them is quite good for checking the spread of disease. It is interesting to note how little things can make a big difference, even in storing potatoes. When I stored mine I had a few bushels more than I could comfortably accommodate, so I filled up a large wooden box in the shed and also a big iron drum. I forget what it was originally used for; it is made of corrugated iron, round like a cylinder, three feet deep and two feet across—we used it for a time as a water-butt. It was quite clean and dry and I filled it up to the top and covered it with a flat piece of tin. You might think potatoes would be happy enough in that, but they are not; half-way down they were quite wet, and that's where I found the bad ones. Those in the box are as right as ninepence, because there are cracks in the bottom of the box which allow air to circulate. It shows how important ventilation is; they haven't been there a month yet, but they were going wrong already, perhaps a few holes knocked through the bottom of the drum will make all the difference.

Brussels sprouts are turning in nicely now, unless the caterpillars have ruined them, which I'm afraid is the case in some places, and there is a good deal of moaning going on about it. Candidly, I have very little sympathy with it. A timely application of derris would have kept them away, and there were plenty of warnings given. Let us hope that the attacks are not too widespread. What I set out to say about brussels is that you can make them last much longer if you gather them properly. I have often seen people stripping all the nice hard little sprouts from the upper half of a stem and leaving the bottom ones because they weren't quite so solid and nice. That is sheer waste; the way to gather sprouts is to take the lower ones from all the plants, gradually stripping the plants from the bottom upwards all together and picking off the big yellow or fading leaves as you do so. I usually advise finishing off with the tops in the late winter, but last year I tried it the other way round and took the tops early. They get loose and coarse if you leave them till the last, whereas in the autumn they are tight and solid and as hard as a cricket ball. We gathered a few of the lower sprouts and then tried the tops somewhere in late November or early December. They were very good indeed and lasted for weeks, and so far as I could tell it made no difference at all to the development of the sprouts below. I was afraid it might expose them to the weather too much, but it didn't seem to, we only cut the round centre or heart out of the tops which still left plenty of protecting leaves. Mine are late this year, and so far the tops have not hearted up at all, nor the sprouts either for that matter, so I shall have to wait and see.

Very well, let us assume that the cabbages are planted, the leeks and celery earthed up, and all the other odd jobs well in hand—the next thing to tackle is the autumn digging. There is a great advantage in getting the rough digging done in the autumn, and the earlier the better, especially on heavy ground and where there is a lot of rubbish to be buried, and more especially on new land which is at present under turf. Let us deal with that first, because I believe a good many victory diggers are about to take on a new plot of grassland, perhaps the first allotment they have ever tackled, and at first sight it may look a tough proposition. How are we going to set about it? Obviously the first thing is to dig it. We have got to break up the ground as deeply as possible with the turf buried at least a spit deep, and the sooner it is done the better so that the winter can sweeten the soil and the turf will have time to rot down into valuable plant food. If you leave it till the spring it would be too late for that and the turf would have to be taken off and stacked. Now straight digging doesn't agree with some people—I'm afraid I'm one of them. It makes my back ache if I do much of it, but by starting early and taking it easy I can get through it without much difficulty. As a matter of fact, digging is what you make it, it need not be hard work if taken in moderate doses, sensibly and methodically. Some people start off for the first time as if their lives depended on getting it done before tea-time; then, of course, they knock themselves up and finish by calling the spade anything but a spade. If you are not used to it, the best way is to take it quietly, and as soon as your back begins to ache, go and rest awhile or do something else for a change. Then do a bit more later on, gradually increasing as you become accustomed to it. Start by getting a good sharp spade, you can't do good work with bad tools, and having got one that suits you keep it sharp and clean; it makes a surprising difference. You remember when you used to try to carve a joint of beef with an ordinary blunt table-knife and perhaps finished up with the joint on the floor and gravy all over your Sunday trousers? But what a difference when you had a really sharp carving-knife, and you looked round and said, "Anybody have a bit more?" Well there is just as great a difference between digging with a clean, sharp spade and a dirty one. I have often watched Henry digging—he always carried a little wooden scraper tucked in the strap round his leg, and every now and then he would scrape the spade nice and clean. He never hurried, but kept quietly on without over-exerting himself, but he got through a surprising amount of work, and I have often seen him after the job was finished seated on a box filing the edge of the spade and polishing it up with an oily rag before putting it away. A common fault with beginners is that they try to take too much at a time on the spade, and make hard work of it. Cut each spadeful out neatly, not more than six inches at a time, drive the spade in vertically to its full length, and turn it completely over, leaving it like that without chopping it up or trying to leave a neat surface; the rougher you leave autumn digging the better, with plenty of holes and spaces for the frost and snow to get into it. A hard winter on newly dug soil is better than a dose of fertilizer, especially if it can penetrate deeply. But I'm afraid I am getting a little ahead of myself; we were going to tackle that new plot of grassland, and give it its first deep digging. Most likely it is a rectangular piece, so the first thing to do is to divide it into two equal parts, lengthwise, with a dividing mark down the middle. Now across the end of one half measure off a strip two feet wide. Cut the turf into sections with the spade, pieces about a foot square, skim them off, and stack them at the same end of the other half—that will be only a few paces away, but stack them off the actual plot if you can. Next dig out the soil where you have removed the turf, a full spade deep, and place it beside the stack of turf. This will give you your first trench, two feet wide, and the art of digging lies in maintaining a two foot trench right through the digging operation. There will probably be some loose, crumbled soil over the bottom of the trench, shovel this out and throw it on the heap with the other. Then with a digging fork break up the bottom or floor of your trench to loosen it well, but leave the soil where it is. Now measure off the next two feet, skimming off the turf as before, but this time place it, grass downwards, in the trench you have just made, chopping it up with the spade to encourage it to rot quicker. If you like to be thorough it is quite a good plan to sprinkle a little powdered, or more commonly called "whizzed," naphthalene over this turf—it makes it very unpleasant for wireworms and other pests. The next thing is to turn over this strip of soil from which you have just skimmed the turf to fill up the first trench. This is not so easy as it looks, if you just throw it over it will roll back towards you, and soon you won't have any trench left at all, so the best plan is to start at one end of the strip and dig it lengthwise, facing the side of your plot with the trench at your side, not in front of you and working backwards across the plot. Take your first spadeful from the side nearest the grass and away from the trench, turning it over into the side of the trench nearest to you, so that the side of the soil you are now digging will act as a guide and hold it in position for a moment while you pass the next spadeful over beyond it. By this method you will find it much easier to keep to the shape and size of your trench. Shovel out the loose soil from the bottom, throw it over the newly turned soil, and there is your second trench; fork up the bottom as before, then mark off the next two feet, skim off the turf, and proceed as before till you get to the end of the plot with an open trench. Fill this with turf

63

and soil taken from a new trench across the other half, and then dig back up that half till you reach the end you started from, filling in the last trench with the soil and turf taken from the first one. I'm afraid that is rather a long-winded description of a bit of simple digging, and even now I'm not sure that I have made it very clear. If you go to the pictures you may come across a film made by the Ministry of Agriculture which shows this operation in detail very clearly. It is worth following carefully, because a method like this not only makes digging easier, it also makes a much better job of it, and the success of most of the later cultivation depends very largely on that initial digging. You will notice that by this method the top spit is turned completely over, but the lower soil, although broken up, remains where it is. Some of the old-fashioned gardeners still believe in a method of trenching which brings the lower soil to the top and buries the top soil down below. This is quite wrong, except on a very deep and well-cultivated soil, because that raw subsoil may take years of weathering on the surface to make it fit for seed sowing. Where turf is buried in the manner I have described, no manure should be necessary for the first year, unless, of course, the soil is very poor—you have to use your own judgment in these matters—but a dressing of lime spread over the soil after digging, at the rate of half a pound to the square yard, usually does it good—in any case it can't do it any harm. Digging ground which is already under cultivation is the same in principle, except, of course, that you don't have turf to bury, but instead you turn all the weeds, farm manure, if any, or the remains of the compost heap, into the bottom of the trench. As a general rule, fertilizers should not be used during the autumn. Spring is the time for them, and we shall be discussing them in due season. One that is likely to be scarce and difficult is potash, so I would suggest that you start now and save all the ashes you can from wood fires, rubbish or couch fires, anything but coal, and keep them in the dry for use in the spring, because they contain potash. Common soot is excellent too—save all you can, or if you have nowhere to keep it spread it over the garden as you collect it. You can do the same with the ashes, if you like; potash doesn't evaporate like some of the chemicals, and it will still be available in the soil next year. When I said bury the weeds I meant annual weeds such as chickweed, groundsel, and so on, not perennial weeds. Anything with thick creeping roots or tap roots, such as thistles, dandelions, couch grass, ground elder, and the like, should be picked out as the digging proceeds. Any extra time spent in picking out these bits of roots is well repaid by a saving of time in the busy season.

PRUNING FRUIT TREES

The vegetables seem to be looking after themselves fairly well for the moment, so I am going to talk about pruning fruit trees. I suppose there are more conflicting opinions written and spoken about pruning fruit trees than about any other subject under the sun, except, perhaps, politics. The fact is that pruning is a rather complicated business, and you can't apply a simple set of rules. It needs common sense and adaptability to suit the method to the condition and circumstances. The idea that an annual snipping all over a tree with a pair of secateurs is going to make a better tree of it, and produce more fruit, is about as sensible as cutting off your finger to cure indigestion. In my opinion there is too much pruning done by enthusiastic amateurs, and many of the trees would be better left alone. I went to see a lady not long ago who showed me a row of neatly trimmed apple trees with large

65

dense heads that you couldn't see daylight through, and she complained that she got very little fruit. What annoyed her most was the fact that the man next door did practically nothing to his trees, but got better crops than she did, although she had a man in once a year to prune hers properly—or at least, that is how she put it—but it didn't occur to her to draw the obvious conclusion from it. Pruning is, of course, desirable, every gardener knows that, but it is, or should be, done with a very definite object in view, either to build up a good shapely tree to produce less fruit and more growth, or to check growth and produce more fruit, and obviously no single method can meet all these requirements. The great danger to fruit trees is haphazard, purposeless pruning or trimming, and I always say that unless you have a good idea why you are cutting a shoot, it is better to leave it alone—there should always be a definite object in view. Forgive me if I am too elementary, but let us first look at the different types of apple trees we've got—the trained types and the free growers. Of the free growers we have the bush, the half-standard, and the standard, the only difference being in the length of the main stem. A standard has a main trunk six or seven feet high, with the tree on the top of it; the half-standard is the same but with a main stem half the length, and the bush has a main stem only about a foot or eighteen inches high. The principal trained trees are the cordon, a single stem without branches, the espalier, an upright central stem with a number of horizontal branches, the fan-trained shape like a fan, usually planted on walls, and several other fancy shapes, such as double and triple cordons, all of which have to be kept to their original shapes, and restricted in size, so obviously the pruning of them is different from that of a tree which is allowed to grow freely. The different forms are usually decided by the nurseryman before we get them, and we have to carry on the good work afterwards. They all have their uses in various planting schemes, as you can easily imagine, but we will take only one of each—the bush tree which I consider the most suitable for large gardens, and the trained cordon which is the most useful for the small garden where space is the main consideration. Let us assume that we have planted a bush tree, which is a small affair, with a number of young shoots radiating more or less from the top of its short central stem. These shoots will form its main branches as it grows up, so it is important that we should try to guide them in the direction needed to build up a shapely and permanent framework. As a rule, when you look at a drawing or diagram of a young tree, it sends out its new branches at regular intervals all round, and the whole thing looks as easy as shelling peas. In actual life they don't always do that, they are just as likely to send two or three fat shoots in one direction and none in the other, and so on. Your new bush tree may have three or four or more healthy young shoots on it when it's planted. If you cut these shoots half-way back, what will happen? In the spring the buds below your cut, or some of them, will break out into more new shoots, that is always the result of cutting a shoot—more like it the next year—unless, of course, you cut it off right at the bottom, leaving no buds at all. Before you cut a shoot you should note the position of the buds and cut just above a bud which points outward so that its new shoot will go in that direction. Some of the lower shoots next year may grow towards the middle of the tree, if so, you cut them right off. You usually get too many, so you cut off all the surplus ones, especially those which are pointing the wrong way. Each year you repeat this process, gradually building up the framework of a tree, open in the centre, with the branches well spaced out all round. When you have reached that stage you change your tactics and prune to

67

get fruit, which often means very little pruning at all beyond a little annual thinning to prevent overcrowding. If you continue the building up process too long you will merely produce a thicket of useless growth instead of a fruitful tree, and this is exactly what many novices do. Let us look at one of these young shoots and see how it normally behaves. If you cut it, the buds on the piece you leave will break out into new shoots. But suppose you leave it alone, what happens then? Most likely it will grow a little at the end, but not much, and the lower buds will begin to develop into fruit spurs. These will soon absorb most of the energy producing fruit, while growth at the end will gradually stop. You have to decide then, whether you want fruit or more new shoots. Now look at an ordinary branch on a full-grown or well-established tree. You don't quite know what you will find, it depends on the condition of the soil, age, and previous treatment of the tree. You may find a few fruit spurs and a whole lot of young shoots which have grown during the summer. There is no point in multiplying these, so what I should do is to cut off some of them completely, right at the bottom, to thin them out, and leave the others alone. Again you might find a lot of fruit buds and spurs, but only a few new shoots. In that case I should cut them back leaving about six inches at the bottom of each, because you need a certain amount of new growth to stimulate root action. You might even find no new shoots at all, but a whole lot of spurs and buds. This may mean that the tree has had little or no previous pruning, has settled down to the fruiting habit, stopped growing, and will soon approach the starvation period. In this case it is better to thin out the spurs and cut back some of the strongest side shoots which may be a year or two old, or if there are none, cut a little off the end of the branch to induce new growth, and give the tree a barrow-load of manure, or a handful of sulphate of

68

ammonia in the spring. This condition, when growth has stopped, usually means either semi-starvation or, more likely, that the tree has never been pruned. Remember then, that if a tree is regularly pruned it will keep on producing new growth, even an old tree, but, if not pruned at all, it will gradually check its own growth, and finally stop growing altogether and produce only blossom and fruit which will gradually deteriorate. So you have to strike the happy medium. One other point, nearly every branch on a fully grown tree has a leading shoot at the end of it. This end shoot, as a rule, should be left alone. There are exceptions, I know, when it benefits by light pruning, but more often than not cutting it does more harm than good. I'm afraid all this sounds rather complicated; if this were television I daresay I could explain it easier, but actually you can boil it all down to a fairly simple process. If you have a good healthy tree forget the word pruning and call it thinning. Thin out the young growth in the middle of the tree so that the main branches are clear. Thin out an entire branch here and there if there are too many of them crowded together. If you can throw your hat right through the middle of the tree, if you can sit in the branches and get a clear view between the leaves in every direction, then the sunshine will penetrate and you will get fruit. Remember this, that if a youngish tree is growing very strongly, as they sometimes do on rich soil, pruning the shoots won't stop it, it will make it grow stronger and denser. Leave it alone, and give it no manure of any kind, sow grass or flowers underneath it to use up some of the strong food. If, on the other hand, it refuses to grow at all but bears a lot of blossom and a few scrubby little apples, the remedy is severe pruning in conjunction with feeding. Remember, too, that in the case of a young tree the wise gardener aims at building up a healthy tree first, and getting the fruit afterwards. You sometimes see a tiny tree, perhaps in its first year, with three or four fine apples on it. Very pretty too! It makes a nice photograph, but it may take the tree years to get over it, and perhaps throw it out of gear for ever. You can't have it both ways—be patient and reasonable and don't allow blossom to develop until the tree is at least three years old. If you have a tree less than seven years old, which is making very strong growth but doesn't seem inclined to fruit, dig it up, trim back one or two of the strongest roots a little and plant it again, not deeply but firmly. This often has the desired effect. You can't do that with an older tree, but you can dig down about a yard from the trunk and cut off one or two of the roots. This gives it a check and often induces it to start fruiting.

Finally, a word about the trained tree—the cordon, for instance, which is just a straight stem without any branches and is never allowed to grow into a big tree at all. Here we are up against something different, we are producing and maintaining an unnatural tree, and have to resort to unnatural methods to do it. Perhaps you are planting a few cordons now; if so, they may have been pruned by the nurseryman, and you need do nothing for the moment. If they haven't cut off all the side shoots to within two inches of the main stem, cut just a little, only a few inches, off the leading shoot at the end. In the spring more shoots will begin to sprout out all along the stem, and another leading shoot to continue the length of it; this is usually called the leader, and the side shoots are called laterals. In July these laterals will probably be a foot long. At that time you cut them all back to about half their length, the top bud soon breaks out into a new shoot to take the place of the piece you cut off, but the cutting process has checked the flow of sap which has a tendency to congregate for a time in the lower buds and convert them into fruit buds. At this time of the year you cut off the whole lateral leaving only a stump with not more than three buds on it. These will very likely form fruit spurs, but if you had missed the summer cut they would most likely break out in the spring as new shoots. You don't cut the leading shoot in July, but now you shorten it a little, leaving eighteen inches to lengthen the tree by that amount each year till it reaches the height you want. Then you stop cutting the leader altogether. Each branch of an espalier, or other trained tree, is treated in the same way as a cordon; this method is known as spur pruning or double pruning. How simple it all seems, doesn't it? And if trees would all behave alike, it would be, but, unfortunately, they don't, and the art of pruning lies in studying and understanding their funny little ways and treating them accordingly. An ounce of common sense is worth a ton of theory if we would only learn to use it.

December

COLLECTIVE EFFORTS

I WONDER how much extra food we have grown in the country this year as a result of the Dig for Victory campaign. Very difficult to say, I'm afraid, but the increase must have been substantial. But this is no time for looking back and resting on our laurels, we have got to put our backs into it from now onwards and do better still—a great deal better in some districts. In the urban and industrial areas the allotment movement has grown to such an extent that in some places the difficulty now is to find land to satisfy the demands, and some enthusiastic gardeners I know of have to travel long distances after the day's work to get to their allotments. This is a great pity, but I suppose it can't always be avoided. Taking it all round, I think the large industrial centres are pulling their weight very well; there are exceptions, of course, where the drive and enthusiasm is lacking in official circles, but they aren't many. It seems to me—mind you this is only my view—that we ought now to look to the country villages to get a move on and produce far more food than they have ever done before, not merely for themselves, but also for those who are unable to grow anything. There are still plots of good ground, I know of, producing nothing but rubbish, vacant allotment plots, derelict gardens, and odd bits of land, which all over the country would mount up to thousands of good fertile acres, and by hook or by crook we should get this land cultivated. I am often told that local authorities have power to take over such land; that may be, and if it were two or three acres in once piece they might be able to do something about it, but when that two or three acres is scattered about in little oddments all over a parish, it is a different story, and I have a feeling that the only way to get it done is to offer some direct inducement for the villagers themselves to cultivate it, to make it worth their while. The position at the moment is that most of the villagers grow enough food for their own use and make the village self-supporting as far as vegetables are concerned, and so long as they do that everybody seems quite satisfied. But I maintain that they could do more than that—not everywhere, of course—but in favourable districts. Properly organized they could make a substantial contribution towards the food supply in the towns, but it would have to be done collectively. It is no use waiting for a sort of accidental surplus of odds and ends of perishable summer vegetables, like beans, cauliflowers, or brussels sprouts, and then trying to find a market for them. I think the word "surplus" is rather misused. I am often told by the powers that be that there is no evidence of any surplus production in the villages. Of course there isn't, because at present there is so little known of any inducements for them to produce it. But suppose villagers knew they could get the guaranteed price for all the onions and shallots they grew in addition to their own requirements, I believe we could double the output, and the markets would be very glad to get them. As a matter of fact, the National Vegetable Marketing Company, which has been established under the Ministry of Food to buy vegetables, will, if it is requested to do so, and wherever practicable, purchase onions and carrots from growers in gardens or allotments on less than an acre of agricultural land, provided the produce is put together in lots of one ton and upwards. That, I think, is worth knowing. But all this wants organizing. I believe it's now the job of the County Garden Produce Committees, and in some counties these are working well, but like so many things, I think you have really got to start at home.

Now have you even got a local horticultural society in

your village, and do you work as a community or as separate individuals? Many villages have such a society, and they are doing good work; some have tried to form one, have made a half-hearted start and then it's fizzled out, others have never tried. Well, now is the time to be getting busy or we shall miss the boat again and be too late. It is all a question of local leadership. In practically every village there is someone who has the ability to organize, the gift of leadership, and I appeal to them now to waste no more time, but to use all their efforts to form a local garden society, and, having formed it, to keep it alive. What are the advantages? Perhaps I can best answer this by telling you something of what has been done in a little village in the Midlands. It is quite small, with a population of about 300, very much like a thousand other villages up and down the country. About this time last year a few influential people decided to form a local horticultural society so they called a meeting and fixed up the preliminaries. Perhaps they (or shall I say we, because I was there?) were very fortunate in the choice of a secretary, one who possessed the gift of leadership, was popular, and had the happy knack of rubbing people up the right way instead of the wrong, and he very soon roped in nearly every man in the village. This choice of a secretary, I may say, is the crux of the whole business. The success of a society depends almost entirely on the secretary, he can either make or mar it. Too often at these initial meetings somebody proposes old Bill Smith, perhaps because he is a good dart player, or enjoys some sort of cheap popularity, fine fellow, perhaps, but about as suitable for a secretary as a blind donkey. Perhaps someone seconds him and he is elected before anyone has given serious thought to the matter. "All right," he says, "and thank you. I don't know much about such things, but I'll do my best." No doubt he does, but it doesn't get you far. I cannot emphasize too strongly the importance of getting the right type of man, or woman, for this job. It must be someone who is not merely interested, but who can lead and not follow. Well, as I said, *we* had a good one, and we soon got down to the real job of digging for victory on co-operative lines. We bought over thirty-five pounds worth of small seeds wholesale, nearly seven tons of Scotch seed potatoes, and two or three tons of lime and other things, and I calculate that on these items alone the members not only got their shilling subscription back, but were, on an average, two or three shillings in pocket on the deal. It meant a good deal of work in distribution, but willing hands made light work, and they enjoyed doing it. Then we developed a social side to it; so many of these local societies peter out through lack of interest when the first wave of enthusiasm cools down, and we decided we must keep the members together. So we started monthly meetings in the village hall, which included talks, discussion, coffee and biscuits, and sometimes even a song or two, and the members soon began to look forward to these gatherings, and although we dropped them in the summer they are going strong again now. In the spring some of us felt ambitious and decided to hold a show; there was a good deal of discussion about it, some for, some against, but the ayes had it, and so it came to pass. There hadn't been a show in the village for at least forty years, and that wasn't much of a success, so there were plenty—as there always are in any village—who shook their heads and prophesied the worst. Some thought it wrong and a waste of time to hold a show in war-time. I wonder how you feel about it? Personally, I think that so long as a show is run on sensible lines in the right spirit, and at the right time, there is everything to be said for it. Gardeners as a class are good wholesome people, they love to get together and discuss their triumphs and their failures.

75

They are very much like invalids in that sense, they
argue for hours over an onion and thoroughly enjoy themselves. They like to brag and show each other what they
can do, and go one better than somebody else. The show is
a great occasion for a gathering of the clans, a day of
reminiscences. It brings a bit of light and pleasure to
what otherwise is rather a drab routine. We all know the
enormous value, the refreshing influence of the Ensa
concerts to the troops, and the lunch-hour entertainments
in the munition factories; the local flower and vegetable
show brings the same happy influence to the diggers for
victory—it keeps the men up to scratch and makes them
do even better. Of course a show can be run on the wrong
lines; for one thing, it can be held too early. A good many
were held in July this year, and some of the men dug up
several rows of immature potatoes or other crops in the
hope of finding a dozen good ones for a show. That of
course means waste, and we oughtn't to encourage it. Anyway, we decided to hold a show. At first our ideas were on
very modest lines, vegetables only in the village hall
sometime in September. Then came a plea for flowers; for
the Women's Institute to join in; for a few side shows and
sports to entertain people and raise a little money. And
why not a band? If we could get one for nothing! Sounds
ever so much better than a gramophone relayed through
loud speakers. And what about refreshments? The
Women's Institute was quite willing to undertake that
side of it. And so the ideas gathered momentum. We
published a souvenir programme. I thought 200 would be
ample, but we were persuaded to order a thousand; they
cost £27, and we got £36 for advertisements, and they were
all sold a fortnight before the show. We held the show in
the private grounds of the local mansion and ordered a
huge marquee which rather frightened us when it was put
up—it seemed as vast as a cathedral, and I think the poor

old secretary had a sleepless night or two wondering how he could collect enough stuff together to make it look full, but when the day came we had to squeeze the exhibits up a bit to get them all in. I never saw so much enthusiasm, the members of the committee worked like navvies in their limited time, clipping, mowing, and generally preparing for the great day. And when it came, the sun shone on our labours and on the uniforms of the local Home Guard and their brass band. The marquee was packed with produce which brought very high compliments from official quarters. The crowd rolled up in vast numbers, goodness knows where they came from. The Women's Institute members were overwhelmed by the hungry and thirsty, and soon sold out what they had regarded as vast and impossible quantities. We had auction sales and competitions, and everybody was thoroughly happy. I didn't see a single quarrel all day. And the result? We sent £120 to the Red Cross Agricultural Fund and a lorry load of vegetables to a local Army unit, and fired all the gardening fraternity with so much enthusiasm that they are still talking about it and making plans for next year. I admit that we were favoured with certain special advantages which would not be available to all villages (for one thing, the B.B.C. came to broadcast the show, and that proved a great attraction), but given the necessary courage and foresight most villages could put up as good a show as we did. Now just in case you think I am boasting, I ought to say that I am not the secretary. I was merely one of the helpers who hung around and did as he was told. As a direct result of forming our little society we have brought into cultivation several allotment plots which have been derelict for years, all the members have worked well together, and I think I can safely say that at least an additional ten tons of valuable food has been produced in the village, and there are more fat pigs in the sties than there have been for a long time. We are now working out schemes for next year and hope to do better, and I hope you will have a shot at it in your village too. If we all pull together and do our best we can add many, many tons of good food to the nation's larder for next winter. So, Go To It!

NOTES FROM THE POST-BAG

I spent the best part of yesterday sorting over my post-bag and reading some of the letters which have accumulated during the week. I should be a very clever man if I could answer all the questions that are sent to me nowadays, and even if I *were* clever enough I could never find time to deal with half of them, so I have selected a few which seem to be of sufficient general interest to be dealt with over the microphone, and I warn you, you are in for a penn'orth of mixed to-day instead of a straight talk on one subject. To begin with here is one about the lawn, one of many like it, asking me what is the best treatment for the lawn during winter. I suppose the obvious answer just now is, dig it up and get it ready for a crop of vegetables in the spring. I expect that will be the fate of a good many lawns this winter but, even so, I hope we shall be able to grow enough food without scrapping every blade of grass in the garden. There is no excuse for big lawns just now, but there is every excuse for maintaining a little one, and if we do we may as well make the best of it and keep it in good condition. It is rather the same with the flower border; I find a good many people who seem to think it wrong to grow flowers in war-time so they have just neglected them and allowed the border and the lawn to run to waste and get overgrown with weeds. I'm afraid I can't see anything patriotic in that. Let us have it one way or the other; if you decide to dig up the lawn and flower garden and grow vegetables on it, so much the better, but if you are not growing food on it there is no sense in letting it become an eyesore and a nuisance to others, you might just as well keep it neat and tidy and enjoy the flowers. I'm afraid, after all, it is a question which each one must decide for himself or herself. But to return to the lawn. Should it be mown, rolled, and fed during the winter or left alone? Many people put away the mower for the winter but keep the roller active; I prefer it the other way round, continuous rolling during wet weather, especially on heavy ground, consolidates the soil till it is like concrete, and does more harm than good, but an occasional light mowing with the machine set high during mild weather does it good. A good lawn is made up of various types of grasses, some strong and tufty which continue to grow in the winter, others fine and delicate which don't, and if the coarse ones are allowed to grow unchecked they gradually smother and choke the finer ones, and the quality of the turf deteriorates. An occasional light mowing without the box prevents this. But neither mowing nor rolling nor anything else should be done to a lawn during frosty or snowy weather. This is a good time to patch up a lawn with new turf, but not a good time to feed it—March is soon enough for that. If moss is prevalent it should be raked out as much as possible and a dressing of hydrated lime given, at the rate of half a pound per square yard. Worm casts can be scattered about during dry weather with a hard broom, but if they're very numerous one of the advertised worm killers will soon reduce them. Talking about turf, allotments holders digging new grassland often ask me whether the turf should be buried or stacked in a heap on one side. Well, if your digging is done before Christmas I should say bury the turf, but in the spring I would rather stack it or, better still, make use of it as building material. Nicely cut turves make quite good walls and you can build a square bin with them to put the compost or rubbish in, and then next autumn chop down the whole lot, turf and compost together for digging into the ground. You can build quite a good garden frame, too, with turf, I don't know if you have ever tried it; all you need is a light to put over the top, and you can raise all sorts of spring seedlings in it, and finish up with a couple of marrow plants for the summer. Even so, the best plan is to get the digging done before Christmas and bury the turf well below.

A correspondent tells me that he invested in a set of glass cloches, the continuous kind for covering rows of early vegetables and strawberries, and he wants to know if they can be put to any use during the winter. Of course, they can—to a very good use, too—provided that he has the vegetables already sown or planted. Many of the crops such as winter lettuce, spring cabbage, autumn-sown onions, broad beans, peas, and parsley, simply mark time, and look rather sorry for themselves during the winter. It is not so much the cold weather in this country that keeps things back as the continuous wet conditions. A row of onions, for instance, covered with cloches now will be ready for use as spring onions much earlier. Parsley will continue to grow, broad beans and early peas, young cauliflowers, lettuces, and even spring cabbages will do much better under the protection of these cloches. Stand an odd one or two over a root of mint and you will get it much earlier. You can also use them on flowers, such as pansies or forget-me-nots and others, to get them earlier and better. There is just one important thing to remember; if you put a row of these cloches along a row of vegetables, like a sort of tunnel, you must close up the ends with a sheet of glass or a board or something, otherwise you'll get a cold draught through them which will do more harm than good.

While we are on the subject of glass, I often get letters

80

from listeners who have an old grape vine in a greenhouse and want to know how and when to prune it. You can prune it now, and the sooner it's done the better, and it is a perfectly simple operation. You merely retain the main rods or branches of the vine and cut everything else off, leaving nothing but a number of long bare branches with knobs on. In the spring young shoots sprout out from these main branches, and on these young shoots the grapes are produced. The usual system is to allow one bunch of grapes to set on each of these side shoots, and then pinch the end of it to prevent it growing longer. The bunch is usually cut with a piece of the shoot attached to it, nice and handy to carry it with, and in the autumn the remainder of the shoot is cut off close to the main branch, or rod, as gardeners call it, leaving only one bud or eye, and you get back more or less to the starting-point again, starting each spring with a new crop of side shoots springing more or less from the same place. If you've allowed too many long rods to develop cut the weakest of them out, leaving only enough to make a convenient framework to carry each year's crop. There's a good deal more than that in growing good grapes, of course, but that is a brief outline of the pruning system. The pruning of indoor peaches is also quite simple. You cut off the old shoots which bore the peaches in the summer and train a young one into their places. These young ones which have grown this year will bear the peaches next, so out with the old to make room for the new—that's all it amounts to. If it is a healthy tree there will probably be more young shoots than you want, if so, cut some of them out, keeping if possible the one which springs from the lower end of the old shoot you are cutting off. To put it another way, the shoot which bore the peaches may have a number of young shoots along it. Cut it off, complete with its young shoots, just above the lowest one, nearest the main branch, and bend that down to take the place of the one you have cut off. Of course, a lot of these surplus young shoots ought to have been pinched off during the summer out of the way of the peaches, but it's no use talking about that now. Another greenhouse question which frequently crops up is how often to water geraniums, fuchsias, and other plants in pots? This is a difficult question to deal with in a general way. It depends on the temperature, and whether the plants are growing or resting. As a rule plants require very little during the depths of winter. Geraniums and fuchsias which are resting are better without any water at all between now and March, especially if they are in a cool house. If I had sixpence for every geranium which has been killed with cold water in the winter I would buy Lord Beaverbrook a whole fleet of tanks. When a plant is resting it doesn't want water. On the other hand, you may have a batch of cyclamen or primulas or cinerarias which are growing in a warmish house and soon going to flower. They need water, but only when they are dry, not once a day whether they need it or not. Make sure that the soil is dry and that the pot rings hollow when you tap it, then fill them right up. Dribbling a little on the top every day does more harm than good, it makes them look wet when perhaps the roots are dry, or else it keeps them too wet. Generally speaking, when a plant is actively growing or flowering and the pot is full of roots, it needs a fair amount of water; when it is doing nothing it needs little or none, and this applies to all plants whether in rooms or the greenhouse. The worst thing of all is to keep the pots in saucers filled with water, they don't like it.

A lady tells me she is constantly trying to grow mustard and cress in boxes in her small greenhouse but it nearly always goes mouldy instead of growing, except during the summer when she can manage it quite nicely, but doesn't need it then. I have heard it said that it takes a good gardener to grow mustard and cress all the year round; it isn't the easiest thing in the world, especially in small cold or half-heated greenhouses where the atmosphere is dead and stagnant, because the weather is too cold or foggy to open the ventilators—that is the enemy—damp. If you can maintain a buoyant atmosphere with a circulation of fresh warm air you can grow mustard and cress easily enough, but not without. Watering is important, too, if you keep dribbling water over it during the winter it is almost sure to damp off. It should have a good soaking to start with when you sow it, and then no more if you can possibly avoid it. But if it does become necessary, it is better to hold the box in water and let it soak up from below. Mustard and cress is very acceptable as a winter salad; a fairly warm living-room which keeps warm at night, or a linen cupboard, or the bathroom is a good place if you are allowed to use it. The simple way is to fill a seed box three parts full of finely sifted soil and soak it well with absolutely boiling water. This helps to sterilize it. Let it drain, and then sow the seed thickly all over it, and gently press it into the soil with a flat iron or something; then cover it with a sheet of glass or brown paper. This helps it to germinate evenly, but you must remove the covering as soon as the seeds begin to shoot. The warmer it is the quicker, of course, but don't water it overhead at any time. It must have a certain amount of daylight, of course, after it has germinated, but not necessarily sunshine. There is really no need to grow cress, unless your palate is a very discerning one—white mustard alone is quite good, but if you prefer the two, keep them separate, and sow the cress three days before the mustard, then they will be ready together. Mixing the seed is the cause of many failures. That brings us to other seeds, and one listener complains that when he buys a shilling packet of seeds from his favourite seedsman there is more in it than he requires; he still has a good many half-packets

83

left. Will they be worth keeping for sowing in the spring? As to the first part, people don't often complain that they get too much, usually the other way about, but the remedy is in the hands of the seedsman, either to put less in the shilling packet or make sixpenny or threepenny packets. For the second part, I would much rather have new seed, but I should certainly keep last year's in case some things happen to be short. I think there will be plenty of the essentials to go round, but you never know, and some of the vegetable seeds will keep sound and good for several years, but it is a bit risky.

MORE STOCKTAKING

We shall very soon see the end of 1941, and good riddance to it! I shall be happy to start on a new diary and happier still to see the days begin to get a bit longer. I suppose, as a gardening year, it hasn't been too bad. We have had failures, but I think most of us have had our successes too, and this is a very good time to take stock of the results and see if we can cut out the failures next year and resolve to do better than we've ever done before. I've just been looking through my notebook and I find that, even after a good many years' experience, I still make mistakes, especially in the balancing of crops. I should think one of the most difficult things in cultivating a vegetable garden or allotment is to plan so as to get just enough of everything and not too much of anything. Let us have a look at some of my own results. For one thing, I had too many early potatoes, half a dozen long rows, and they did very well, but we couldn't eat them all while they were in the new potato condition, and that, I take it, is the main reason for growing earlies—to get succulent new potatoes: they don't crop so heavily as the maincrops, and there is no point in growing them to maturity or in keeping them.

There are people, of course, who don't like them too young, they prefer them when they get a bit older and cook floury. I like new potatoes small and soft and melting, and I think most people do; they may be considered luxuries in wartime, but I cannot help that, I like luxuries. So the idea should be to spread the supply of new potatoes over as long a period as possible. Assuming that your rows are thirty feet long, and there are only two of you, my suggestion would be two rows of a first early, such as May Queen or Duke of York, two rows of a second early, say Eclipse, and then a couple of rows of one of the early maincrops, such as Majestic or King Edward. These must be extra to your maincrop, specially planted for lifting young before they are fully grown. That means that you will be eating fresh new potatoes from early July till well into September, and you'll have had enough by then. It is not generally known that some of the maincrops lifted half-grown are as delicate and nice as the first new potatoes, and so long as you plant them for that purpose there is nothing extravagant about it, they don't cost any more than the earlies, not so much as a rule. By the way, if you are working out quantities, you can average them out at 7 lbs. of seed for two thirty foot rows, and you won't be far out. If you haven't bought your seed potatoes yet, get them without further delay, or you may be caught napping; some of the popular varieties are already getting short.

I rather overdid the autumn cabbages, they call them harvest cabbages in my part of the country; they make a very good standby, but it's very difficult to get the right quantity. If you plant one row, half of them go wrong, and if you plant two rows, they all mature perfectly and you don't want them, because you've got plenty of cauliflowers. Next year I shall plant one row of Winningstadt, just in case we need them, and during the summer I shall sow a couple of rows of the little hardy coleworts: I like them

85

better than big cabbages. My favourite greens are brussels sprouts and cauliflowers; I never seem to get too many of them. This year I tried a good bed of winter broccoli, but they haven't been worth the bother; a nice white broccoli makes a very acceptable dish during the late winter and spring, when you get it. I can tell other people how to grow them, but I'm bothered if I can make much of a success of them myself: I get on very well with the purple sprouting, but there is something about my garden which doesn't suit the big-headed white ones. Last year I got tremendous plants with a head about the size of a cricket ball in the middle of each, and this year's lot don't look much more promising; I think I shall drop them and grow more brussels sprouts and leeks instead, they are more obliging.

We ought to grow more leeks next year, if we can get seed. I think the public taste for leeks must be increasing, I saw a queue lined up to pay fourpence each for them, but when we could get a big bundle of them for fourpence nobody wanted them—truly we are a strange people. The older I get the more I realize how difficult it is to give advice on cropping an allotment; allotments and gardens are individual things, not all alike, any more than people's tastes are, and you can't generalize or lay down any one scheme to be applied to all allotments. It's no use, for example, including parsnips in the cropping plan if you don't like parsnips. On my table I have quite a number of different leaflets showing how to crop an allotment; they are published by various authorities, and although they differ a good deal in detail, they are all good, and I have no fault to find with them, but I do suggest that you shouldn't slavishly follow any one of them in every detail. So many people, I find, religiously copy these ideas and then they find they have grown a lot of things they don't want. You must use your common sense, get the essence of a good scheme, think it over carefully, and adapt it to your own circumstances and requirements, grow more of the things you like, and less or none of the things you don't like, so long as you bear in mind the importance of food values. None of us can tell another man or woman what they ought to like; you describe a certain vegetable as delicious, and to you it is so, but it doesn't follow that other people are going to like it too. You either like a thing or you don't, you can't control your tastes. Admittedly, some people don't like a certain vegetable because they have never had it properly cooked or presented, but that is another story. What I am warning you about is that if I should happen to rhapsodize over a particular vegetable and call it lovely, well, try it by all means, but don't go all out for it till you have; you might not agree with me. Last year I had a lot to say about the new sugar pea called Paramount; this is a heavy cropping pea which produces large full pods, but you don't shell them, you cook and eat pods and all. There is no stringiness about them, they are very sweet and melt in your mouth rather like asparagus and, of course, they are very economical. We like them very much, so I sang their praises far and wide, and got some of my friends to grow them. Strangely enough, they were not at all favourably impressed. One friend grew a row, and had a good crop: he tried a dish of them, pronounced them "slimey," said he wouldn't give twopence a bushel for them, and told me I could have the rest of them, so I had them, which suited me very well, but it just goes to show how widely different our tastes and palates are. As time goes on you will be bombarded with good advice from every quarter, there never was so much good advice flying about as there is now. All I can say is follow it carefully, sift it out well, season it with your own common sense, which is the greatest asset of all in gardening, and adapt it to your own requirements, then you will get the fullest benefit from it.

I think one of the difficulties this year is to work out the correct quantities of seeds: in ordinary times we order an ounce or two of everything and waste about half of it. Seed this year is a bit more expensive, and not only that, good seed may not be any too plentiful, so I think we ought to go a bit easy with it. Start with beans, for instance; half a pint of each type ought to be ample for a ten rod plot if you space them out properly. The dwarf French beans are not always used to their best advantage, because they so often clash with the runners and get neglected. I never can see anything in the craze for getting everything early, especially runner beans. I would rather eat up the dwarfs first, and these, in my opinion, are not much appreciated unless you *do* get them early. Have you ever tried sowing them in pots or boxes in a frame during March and planting them out early in May? It's quite a sound idea. You want an early maturing one such as Superlative, and if you can sow them in small pots, one seed to a pot, they transplant quite well, and you can get them much earlier. You have to protect them on frosty nights, of course, an old bag or two over the frame will do that, and gradually harden them off before planting out, and then pick the beans as soon as they are four or five inches long and cook them whole—you get the real flavour that way—and if you keep them gathered they crop for quite a long time and last till the runners come along in August. Between them they give you a constant supply of beans from late June till the frost comes. I shall try a few rows of the dwarf beans again for harvesting as winter haricots; Masterpiece and Canadian Wonder are good varieties for this job. This year has been a bit disappointing: it was a miserable summer for ripening anything, but we can hope for a better one next year. The mistake many people make with these haricot beans is that they will be tempted to gather the first and best of the pods for eating green during the summer, leaving the later ones to ripen. This is bad policy, because the later ones are not nearly so good, and don't have time to ripen properly. You mustn't gather any in the green state if you want a good crop for drying. If you allow the first crop of pods to develop and ripen you won't, of course, get later beans, or so many as you do if you keep them gathered. For gathering green we usually space the plants out at least six inches apart; there is no need to do that if you are going to harvest them, two inches is enough, and, of course, you sow them in the open ground during May, there is no need to bring them on in frames. Brassica seed is usually wasted a good deal, such plants as cabbage, brussels, cauliflowers, and so on. How many do you want? Or rather, how many are you ordering? There is usually at least a thousand seeds in an ounce, so I should think a quarter ounce or small packet would be plenty of any of them for a ten rod plot. You can get half a dozen thirty foot rows of onions from an ounce of seed if you sow it properly, so why order more? It is the same with practically all the vegetables; there is no need to grumble about the war-time prices, they can't be helped, buy rather less than usual and sow it more sparingly, and you will get better crops. Talking about beans in frames reminds me that very often the garden frame, where there is one, is empty during the summer. Some people grow cucumbers in it, but as often as not it remains idle. Why not grow melons in it by way of a novelty, and have something to swank about? I am often surprised at the large number of people I meet who have never tasted an English melon, and still more are surprised at me when I say that you can grow good ones in a cold frame. Well, I have often done it. There is a variety called Hero of Lockinge, a white-fleshed one, of good flavour, with beautiful white lacing all over it, which grows and fruits quite well in the frame. Of course, you've got to get somebody to raise the plants for you in a warm house in the spring, but that shouldn't be difficult. You plant them in the frame in May, just as you might plant marrows or cucumbers, and give them reasonable care, and you will be very unlucky if you don't get a few really nice melons.

January

PLANNING AHEAD

I SUPPOSE we are still allowed to wish each other a Happy New Year. At any rate, I wish you all a better one than the last, and especially a successful year in the garden, free from slugs and blight and lumbago and all the other little evils which attend our gardening efforts, or, at least, nearly free; we must have a few of the snags if only to provide a contrast, otherwise gardening might become too easy and lose half its thrills. I always think the New Year is a time for optimism; we know that we may have the worst of the winter yet to come, but the days will begin to get longer and, with the increasing daylight, the garden will soon begin to stir in its slumbers, and every little snowdrop, primrose, or violet seems to remind us that nothing can prevent the spring coming, so there is always something to look forward to. In the meantime, as we can't do much out of doors, let us prepare a cropping scheme so that when the busy sowing and planting time comes we shan't have to waste time deciding where to put this and that. It pays to have a system of cropping, and to work to a pre-arranged plan. What so many novices do is to wait till the crocuses are out and the gardening fever asserts itself, then begin to dig in a hurry, and having got a part of the plot dug, out come the seed packets and in go the seeds, more or less haphazard or according to the date of sowing, as shown on the packet rather than the season of maturity. They forget that some of the earlies to be sown are perhaps the latest to mature. Take parsnips, for instance. You can sow them in February, but you don't dig them up till the following winter. The result is, if you are not careful, that when all your early summer crops are used up, you find a few rows of parsnips across the plot which can't be disturbed, and you wish you hadn't put them there at all, because they prevent that piece of ground being cleared for the winter greens. The time to work all that out is now, before you begin, so let us get a pencil and a bit of paper and see what we can do about it.

Perhaps the simplest plan for a beginner is to divide the plot into two halves, putting the potatoes on one half and everything else on the other half. This is not a perfect plan, but it has its advantages. For instance, potatoes don't like fresh lime, but they do like plenty of manure, whereas many of the other crops respond well to lime, but not to fresh manure, so we can manure the potato half each year and lime the other half. Then the potatoes always get the lime second-hand and the others get the manure second-hand, which is very convenient. Even so, a little more detail is necessary even in the simplest plan. For instance, you would start at the end of your potato patch with the main crops with the earlies adjoining the other crops. Next to the early potatoes you could start with early things like spinach, peas, broad beans, lettuces, small carrots, and then the later things such as parsnips, celery, runner beans, swedes, and others which have to remain till the late Autumn. So you have late potatoes at one end of the allotment and late other vegetables at the other, with all the early summer stuff together in the middle, so that when you've lifted the early potatoes and used up the early summer peas, beans, spinach, and such like, you will have a nice space cleared ready for planting out the winter greens. Next year you start at one end with early potatoes and finish at the other with early summer crops; this will split your winter greens into two parts, one at each end of the allotment for that year, but that doesn't matter much. That's what you call a two-year rotation, and it usually answers quite well. But perhaps you don't want to fill half the allotment with potatoes—I don't, for one—so, in that case, you can try a three-year rotation. For this you divide the plot into three sections: potatoes on one—they get the manure; green stuff and peas and beans on the second— they get the lime; and the root crops on the third—they get neither, but you give them a tonic in the way of artificial fertilizers, and that suits them all, and the whole plot gets manure, lime, and fertilizers once in three years and, of course, you change them round each year.

There is still another method of cropping, which I think I like best of all, and that is grouping the crops together according to their season of maturity. This takes a bit of working out, but it's really fairly simple. Here again you divide the plot into three sections, early, mid-season, and late. On the first section, you grow the early maturing crops, that is, those which are used up first during the summer. How many can you think of off-hand? Early peas, broad beans, short carrots, lettuces, radishes, spinach, autumn-sown cauliflowers, shallots, early turnips, and first early potatoes. All these are used up during the summer, in time to clear the section and plant out the winter greens: this is a lot better than planting them between the rows of potatoes as so many people do. Overcrowding never produces good results. It may be that you want to put out the brussels and things before the early crops are all used up; if so, you can plant between them without any harm, because the early vegetables will be used up and out of the way before there is any danger of overcrowding. Thus you get two crops on the first section. On the second section, you put the late summer and autumn crops, spring-sown cabbages, cauliflowers, more peas, round beet, more carrots and turnips, and anything which is likely to be cleared early in September. I put the early main-crop potatoes on this section. I consider that such varieties as Majestic, Great Scot, British Queen, Arran Banner, and other mid-season varieties are the best to grow on the ordinary allotment,

4

they crop heavily and keep well, and you get them all up in September before blight plays havoc with them. It may be a fad of mine, but I never grow the late varieties if I can help it, it's usually such a messy job getting them up; but the main reason is that it enables you to get this second section cleared in September, which is a real advantage, because you can then sow it immediately with a green crop such as rye or vetches, or a mixture of both, to grow during the autumn and winter, and be dug in as green manure in the spring. Turnips are quite good for this job too, because they give you a few boilings of turnip-tops in the spring, and then you dig the rest in. This green manuring is important in these days of scarcity of natural manure because it supplies humus to the soil, and keeps it in good heart, whereas artificials merely supply the chemical plant food without the necessary bulky material, but more about that later. The difficulty is that unless you work to a cropping scheme you don't find it easy to get ground cleared early enough for sowing the green crop; it ought to be in during September to do any good. Very well then, the second section carries a crop of late summer vegetables, and then a crop of green manure. On the third section, you grow all the late crops, onions, root crops, celery, leeks, runner beans, and anything which has to stop there till the late autumn or winter. As these are cleared you trench and manure the ground, or dig in the remains of the compost heap. Next year you change the sections round, moving them forward. Thus number 1 moves to number 2, 2 to 3, and 3 back to 1.

Perhaps we could best explain this with a simple diagram. You've got your pencils there: draw a rough rectangle. That represents your plot. Now divide it into three parts: mark them one, two, and three. That's the first year. Section one has the early crops followed by winter greens. Section two the late summer crops, and section three the late or winter crops. Now draw another rectangle under the first: divide it into three sections, and mark them three, one, two, in that order. Now still another rectangle with the three divisions: mark them this time, two, three, one. You might as well make a fourth while you are at it, and mark the sections one, two, three. Now you will see that the numbers follow each other round until in the fourth year they are back where they were in the first year. Thus you get a complete change of crops, and three years will elapse before they are back on the same ground. Not only that, but the whole plot gets trenched, manured, green manured, and limed, once in three years, with a minimum of labour and expense. I ought to have said that you put the lime on when you clear the early crops ready for the winter greens. You may not see it all very clearly at first, and you may find a few snags. For instance, I can hear somebody asking where the spring cabbages are going. Well, I should put them on the first section with the winter greens, they will stand there for the winter and spring, but you can get them off in time for celery and leeks, which are not planted out till mid-summer. I'm not suggesting that you should follow either of these cropping schemes in every detail—you might think of a better one, more suitable for your own requirements, but take mine as a basis or guide, and adapt it to your own ideas. In any case, work out a plan of some kind; it will save time and make your gardening much easier.

Now a few words to those who are starting at the beginning, and turning up grassland for the first time. We have already discussed the digging operation: the next thing will be to decide on the most suitable crops to grow during the first season. Some pasture land, with a good depth to it, presents no difficulty, provided it was dug early enough, and the turf buried well down below, it may be capable of growing all the crops quite well, and you could apply one

95

of the cropping schemes to it. But there are other kinds of grassland not so kindly disposed, rough, heavy stuff, full of weeds and rubbish, land which needs at least a season to get it into fertile condition. If you are up against that sort of ground it's no use being too ambitious; it's better to be satisfied with a limited number of things which are likely to succeed, than to fail with the things that won't. Some of the land I have seen turned up lately looks pretty hopeless as far as the sowing of small seeds are concerned. Great chunks of heavy-looking stuff, which flatly refuses to break down into a fine surface for the time being. In such cases, I think the best plan is to leave it rough for the winter, break it down as much as possible, and crop it with vegetables which have been raised elsewhere, and can be planted out after they have got safely through their early infancy, instead of sowing seeds directly into the new plot.

Potatoes are a good cleaning crop, and are very useful for breaking up rough ground, and, if I were asked to suggest a variety for the purpose, I should say Kerr's Pink. It may not be one of the choicest potatoes in the dish, but it is a good one, a big strong grower which usually crops well on the heaviest and roughest of soil, and it seems to dodge most of the diseases. You can plant it in rows three feet apart, and it will cover the ground and choke the weeds, and get the ground into good condition for the following crop. Brassicas usually do well on new ground, provided it is well limed. For this crop you can give a dressing of 1 lb. to each square yard a week or two before planting. Of course, you'll need a seed-bed somewhere to raise them, but there is usually enough room in the home garden for that. If not, you can get plants reasonably from a local nursery. I have seen quite good crops of tomatoes grown on newly-broken pasture land, but, of course, they need a sunny and not too exposed position. Leeks are another good crop for planting out, they fit in well after

96

the early potatoes. Onions are a bit of a gamble as a first-year crop, but shallots usually do well if you can get the surface fine enough to plant them. Swedes are a fairly safe proposition, and I have seen some good rows of celery on new ground, but it had to be treated well. You can never be sure what will happen, but on very rough new ground I should make it a rule to plant rather than to sow small seeds. Peas and beans are worth trying, and you may get excellent crops, especially of runners. But for my part, if I were doubtful about it I should drop all the fancy things for the first year, and be satisfied with a good crop of "taters" and greens.

FRUIT ROBBERS

I want to talk about the fruit trees and bushes for a few minutes to-day. They are not very interesting things to look at just now, and it is easy to forget them, but a little attention at this time of the year may save a lot of time and trouble when the busy season comes round, and perhaps make all the difference between a good crop and a bad one. Fruit trees, as you know, are subject to all sorts of troubles in the form of insect pests and diseases. Caterpillars chew up the leaves and ruin the trees for a season, greenflies suck out the life-blood from the young shoots, capsids disfigure the developing apples, and so on. They come like an invading army during the spring and summer, seeming to appear from nowhere, and before we know where we are the trees and bushes are running alive with them. But where are they now? There used to be an old song called "Where do flies go in the winter time?" I don't know whether it was ever satisfactorily answered, but let us see if we can answer it as far as the fruit tree pests are concerned. They are not all alike, of course, but broadly speaking there are many similarities in their lives

97

and habits. We will take the winter moth as a fairly typical example. This is the parent of those little green caterpillars which make such a mess of the apple trees, and sometimes the oaks as well, in the spring. Those on the oaks are not quite the same species as those on the apples, but their habits are very similar. When the caterpillars are fully fed they let themselves down on a thread. I daresay many of you have had one on your hat or your shoulder, so you know what I mean. Having had a good bellyful of apple leaf they feel like an after-dinner nap, so they crawl into a cosy little corner in the turf, or under some rubbish, spin themselves up into a weatherproof jacket or cocoon and go to sleep till the end of the summer. While they are asleep a mysterious change takes place, and when they wake up they must wonder what has happened to them, for instead of being green caterpillars they are little brown moths. So they creep out and have a look round, and soon find others like themselves, then the boys fall in love with the girls, get married, and have a fine old time for a week or two. But it doesn't last long, they are delicate little creatures and can't live through the winter, but they always make provision for the next generation. The lady moth feels the urge to lay a few eggs before she dies, but she doesn't drop them just anywhere. She knows that in the spring they will hatch out into little green caterpillars and will need some young apple leaves to feed on. Unfortunately, she can't fly, her wings are not big enough, so she crawls up an apple tree and along a branch to the twigs where the buds are, there she lays her eggs and glues them to the twigs near the buds, so that when they hatch in the spring the buds will be bursting into leaf and the little caterpillars will find their breakfast all ready for them. Then, having finished her life's work, she dies, and a tom-tit eats her; the eggs are there and there they will remain, till the warmth of spring wakes them into new life again.

It's all a very wonderful game, but how is the gardener going to stop it? He has three chances. First to prevent the eggs being laid; this is not easy, but it can partly be done by putting greasebands, like fly-papers, round the trunk of the tree in September to catch the moth as she crawls up the tree. His second chance is to destroy the eggs on the twigs during the dormant season, and his third, to poison the caterpillars after they have hatched out and are feeding on the leaves. Obviously, the first two are the most satisfactory, because they are preventives, applied before the damage is done, and also applied during the slack season instead of the busy one. It is too late now to talk about greasebands; they were, or should have been, put on the trees in September. If they were they probably caught a good many moths, but they may also have caught a good many falling leaves during the autumn, which can easily form bridges over the sticky surface. Certain moths are still crawling up the trees, so it would be worth while to have a look at these bands, pick off the leaves and stir up the grease a bit. But in spite of the bands, a good many moths manage to get up the trees to lay their eggs: it is thought that the flying male often carries the female with him. In any case, it is fairly safe to assume that there are eggs on the trees, not only of these moths, but of aphis and other destructive insects, and now is the time to do something about it. These tiny eggs are rather a tough proposition, and one of the problems of spraying has always been to find a chemical preparation strong enough to destroy eggs or insects without injuring the trees themselves. Perhaps the best of all known washes for this purpose is that known as tar-oil, or tar distillate winter wash. This is a tarry preparation which you merely add to water, and it makes a whitish emulsion, very much like the well-known disinfectants, and it is not unpleasant stuff to use. You can buy it under various trade names, or simply as tar-oil

99

winter wash. Most horticultural chemists and sundriesmen know what it is and will supply you with one or other of the well-known brands. You simply dilute it with water to the strength of one part of neat fluid to twelve parts of water, or as directed by the makers, and spray the trees thoroughly all over from top to bottom. Drive it well into the crevices of the bark so that no part of the tree escapes, and it will not only destroy eggs and any hibernating insects which may be tucked up in the corners, but it will clean off moss and rubbish, and brighten up the bark. You can spray all the fruit trees and bushes, and while you are about it do the hedges and fences and rose pergolas, anything except evergreens and plants with green leaves on, such as green vegetables, because it burns leaves and tender growth, and must only be used at this time of the year, while the trees are quite dormant. You must choose a quiet day, too; if you try to do it with the wind blowing you'll get it all over yourself and the next-door washing. We don't get many quiet dry days in January so don't miss an opportunity if you get one. You can usually spray up till the middle of February, after that you have to be careful in case the buds are getting tender. I heard recently of a gardener who used it in mistake for another wash in March when the buds were beginning to swell. For some time there was no sign of life and he was afraid he had killed the tree, then, lo and behold, in late May the buds burst out into blossom, and whereas the blossom on neighbouring trees had been cut by a late frost, his escaped and he had a heavy crop, so he thought he had made a useful discovery, that the tar-oil had merely retarded growth and delayed blossoming, and he wonders if he should make it a regular practice? Well, I certainly shouldn't. I consider it much too dangerous an experiment. It might come off once or twice, or even more, but on the other hand it might not. It is better to regard tar-oil winter wash as a purely winter or dormant season wash, and keep it away from tender growth. Don't use it during wet or frosty weather, and while you are about it give the currants and gooseberries a good doing too. I know the difficulties of spraying in ordinary gardens, it means buying a syringe, or borrowing one, or the stirrup pump, but it doesn't take long, and it really is worth while. If I could only manage one spraying operation during the year this would be the one. It may save any amount of trouble during the growing season. There are two nasty fruit pests whose eggs seem to be proof against tar-oil wash, but fortunately you don't find them everywhere. One is the capsid bug, a green insect which punctures the growing apples and sucks the sap out of them, leaving a lot of ugly wart-like marks all over them which quite spoil the look of a good apple. The other is the red spider, a tiny almost microscopic spider, which breeds like fury all over the leaves and sucks the vital sap out of them. You see it at its worst on wall trees in dry summers, when the leaves turn grey and drop off, and the tree looks, and probably feels, very sick indeed. Both capsid and red spider leave their eggs on the twigs during the winter. Only the other day I found thousands of red spider eggs all along the twigs of a peach tree, they are almost too small to see without a glass, but you can often find them if you search carefully, they are red. Unfortunately, tar-oil wash doesn't destroy them, some growers actually maintain that it does them good. This is probably because it destroys certain other insects which naturally prey on the spiders or their eggs. If you have reason to think that your trees are infected with either capsid or spider, the best wash is a petroleum emulsion, sometimes called white-oil emulsion, diluted in the same way as the tar-oil, and sprayed during the first half of February.

A pest which is very destructive to black currant bushes is the big bud. I daresay you know it well enough. It is caused by thousands of tiny little insects called mites, which are too small to be seen with the naked eye. They get into the buds and disorganize them, so that instead of behaving as normal buds, they swell up into round balls and eventually die. You can't do much about them now except pick off and burn every one you can find or, if a bush is badly infested, grub it right out and burn every bit of it. I may be wrong, and I wouldn't care to put it forward as a proved remedy, but I am under the impression that an annual spraying with tar-oil wash goes a long way towards checking the spread of this pest. Certainly where I have given them a good dousing with it the big bud has been much less in evidence but, of course, it might be coincidence. At any rate, it is worth doing if only to keep the bushes free of aphis. I wonder if you had an attack of mildew on the gooseberries last summer? You would know if you did, because American gooseberry mildew is one of the worst of the gooseberry troubles. It covers the shoots and the berries with patches of a greyish substance, almost like fur or felt, and quite spoils the crop. Anyway, have a look at the bushes now, and you may find that the tips of the shoots, or some of them, are twisted or crippled and stained a darkish colour, perhaps only about an inch or so at the ends. This may have been caused by aphis, but it could also be the result of mildew. But whatever the cause, it is a good plan to cut all these crippled tips off now and burn them, don't just let them drop on the ground and leave them there. This prunes the bushes at the same time, and it's about all the pruning a healthy gooseberry bush needs, except perhaps for the thinning out of a few of the older branches. There are a lot of fancy methods of pruning gooseberries, and I daresay there is something to be said for them, but, for my part, I always say that if you keep a bush thinned out enough to get your hands comfortably between the branches and gather the fruit, no further pruning is necessary. The annual cutting back of all the young shoots simply builds up a thicket of unfruitful growth. So if you have to nip the crippled ends off, cut them just below the damage and leave the rest of the shoot intact.

Just a word about suckers before we go. I am often told that fancy varieties of lilac gradually revert to the common lilac. You see the same thing in many flowering shrubs, such as the fancy viburnums, and even fruit trees and roses. You start with a special variety, and in a few years time it has turned into the common or wild type. Any gardener, of course, could tell you the reason for this. It is because the special variety has been grafted or budded on to a common variety and very often young shoots, known as suckers, spring up directly from the root stock, below the point where the bush was grafted or budded. These will, of course, be the common variety, and if allowed to grow they soon take all the energy from the roots, and the variety which was grafted on it gets starved and gradually dies, while the suckers from below flourish and begin to flower. Well, you mustn't let them; every sucker from the base of the plant, whether lilac, rose, plum, or anything else, if it has been grafted or budded, should be chopped out as soon as they are noticed, or they will surely rob the plant and get the upper hand.

THE ELUSIVE ONION

During these dark days when we can do but little out of doors, I think we might, with advantage, discuss some of the principal crops, onions, for example; I suppose a few years ago a talk on onions would have been considered rather amusing. There have been many jokes made about the good old onion, but it's like a good many other things, we fail to appreciate its qualities until it becomes almost unobtainable, and then we sit up and take notice. Undoubtedly the onion is one of the most popular and useful vegetables we grow. No savoury dish is complete without its pungent influence. It is also a very wholesome vegetable, and in spite of its after-effects and other disadvantages we should be very sorry to be without it. It has been said that onions build you up physically but let you down socially; it may be so, but most of us are willing to chance that nowadays. I'm not sure whether the onion is our oldest cultivated vegetable; it must be one of them, for we can trace it back to ancient Egypt, and it has been grown in the Mediterranean area from time immemorial. It is quite likely a native of Egypt and North Africa, but I'm not sure about that. Anyway, the soil and climate of that part of the world give us a fairly good guide as to the kind of treatment it requires under cultivation. A deep, friable alluvial soil, and good harvesting weather are the main requirements, and although we can't control the weather, we can to a large extent provide the right soil conditions, and by a little manœuvring at seed-sowing time, we can take advantage of the best harvesting weather we get in these islands. Harvesting, as many of us learnt by bitter experience last year, is the important factor in successful onion growing. It doesn't matter how well you cultivate and feed, unless you can gather in the crop in good condition at the end of the season, your labour is more or less wasted. There must have been many tons lost during this winter simply because they were not properly ripened and put away in good condition at the end of the season, especially those which were sown out of doors and were left out till well into October. I don't say it was anybody's fault; I'm not giving away any weather secrets now when I say that we had a wet August—it must have been a record—and a wet August is the worst thing that can happen to an onion bed. A wet June is good, but not a wet August; let us hope the weather will be a bit more considerate this year. One thing I am convinced of is that it pays to get onions sown early, to take advantage of the good growing weather in early summer. In my district those which were sown under glass and planted out did much better than those which were sown out of doors, because of that extra few weeks start that they got. It needs a favourable season to grow and harvest a good crop of onions out of doors, especially in the Midlands and the North, and I am all for early sowing where possible, for at least part of the crop. It saves seed, too, and this, I think, is where local Associations can do a useful work, by sowing seeds communally and distributing the plants instead of packets of seed, or, as in the case of my own small society, by arranging with a nurseryman to raise them for us. If you can get young plants three or four inches high and plant them out in April, they have a much better chance and more time to make good bulbs, and no further thinning is required. Moreover, you usually dodge the first attack of the onion fly which seems to attack them in the very early stages. On the other hand, the advantage of sowing in the open is that the thinnings come in handy for salad purposes; some people made quite a lot of money out of them last year, but I think that is about the only advantage.

The preparation of the soil is important, perhaps more so for onions than for any other crop. Depth is the first essential. You can't grow good onions on a very shallow soil, and you don't usually get much of a crop on new land which hasn't had the sub-soil moved about a bit. The root system of an onion is rather different to that of most of the vegetables. Instead of branching and spreading about in the usual way, each individual root is separate, starting from the bottom of the plant and going more or less

straight down like a long piece of string, and they sometimes go down very deep in search of food and moisture,
so that even if the surface soil is dry and hungry, the
onions won't mind much, so long as there is something
good down below. The idea then, is to dig or trench the
ground as deeply as you possibly can—the deeper the
better—and bury all the dead leaves and waste material
in the lower soil; this soon rots down into just the sort of
food onions are looking for. If you can get a load or two of
good manure, work that in too, but keep it at least six
inches below the surface. Common soot, and poultry
droppings, and a sprinkling of a general fertilizer, are all
excellent, but not too near the surface; the idea being that
the soil should get richer as it gets lower so far as this is
possible. Strong food is not necessary while the plants are
in their infancy, let them find it as they grow up. You are
justified in taking a little extra trouble in preparing an
onion bed because onions don't exhaust the soil, and you
can grow them successfully on the same ground year after
year. If this is not convenient, it is better to let them follow
a crop like celery, which has been well fed and has caused
the ground to be deeply worked. Onions like to push their
roots down through a rather firm soil, so, if necessary, it
is advisable to tread it down a bit before sowing or planting, with the object of getting a fairly firm body of soil
with a couple of inches of fine tilth on the top for sowing
or planting. Personally, I don't make a special bed and
stick to it, I prefer to work onions into the rotation scheme,
choosing the best and richest soil available. But then, I
don't go in for outsize exhibition bulbs; I am satisfied with
a crop of smaller or medium-sized ones, and these are not
quite so exacting in their requirements. Most gardeners, I
believe, like to get big bulbs, and to get them big you've
got to prepare well and give them special treatment.

The first job now is to get the bed prepared on the lines

I have indicated and then get the seed down. For indoor sowing I prefer the first half of February; some people sow in January, but it often means that the seedlings are hanging about instead of keeping on the move. Soil for the seed boxes is not very important; any good old sandy potting soil will do, but if you can mix a pinch of superphosphate or fine bone meal with it, the seeds will germinate quicker and better. There is no need to coddle them, even if you have a good heating apparatus—a temperature of from 50 degrees to 55 degrees is suitable. Sow the seed thinly, and then sift a little soil over them through a fine sieve, and press it down just firm, but not hard. As soon as the seeds have germinated nicely and you can see the little crooks coming through, open the ventilators as much as the weather will let you, and don't over-water them. Gardeners who want big bulbs usually transfer the seedlings when they are big enough to handle, to small pots, one to each pot. That is rather too big a job for most of us, but it certainly pays to transplant them to other boxes, putting them about one and a half inches apart, then they will be comfortable till it is time to plant them out. You must gradually increase the ventilation as they get bigger, and finally in April, stand the boxes out of doors for a week or so before you plant them out. Onions should be planted from six to nine inches apart, in rows a foot apart, and it is important not to plant them deeply, otherwise you get a lot of thick necks. So long as they will stand up, the shallower they are the better. I like to stick a trowel into the soil, pull it forward and drop the roots down behind it, then close it up and make it firm. After that it is largely a question of hoeing and feeding, but we must deal with that later on. I daresay all this sounds a fiddling business, but you would be surprised at the trouble some gardeners take to get those big fat onions you see at the shows. I believe they sit up half the night with them sometimes. But for our ordinary garden and allotments you don't really need exaggerated specimens, and you can usually get a good crop of small but quite serviceable onions without all this trouble, provided you get a reasonably good harvesting season. What I usually do myself is to sow out of doors in late March or early April, and sow the seed very thinly, then leave these undisturbed and let them grow in their own sweet way, except, perhaps, for pulling a few out here and there for use in salads. Onions left unthinned don't seem to get the fly nearly so badly as those which are constantly being pulled about, and you finish up with a nice crop of small or medium-sized bulbs which are just as acceptable in the kitchen as big ones. Just one other point, onion seed germinates better in firm soil than it does in loose soil, so after sowing it is a good plan to run the garden roller over the ground, or tread it down a bit with the feet, if you possess a pair of normal feet and know how to use them. Let us hope we shall all get good crops this year. I have ordered an ounce of Bedfordshire Champion, and I shall feel much happier when I see their little green loops peeping through the soil again. I shall know that another winter is over.

Before I change the subject there is one point of interest to flower show committees. At nearly all the shows I visited last year there were two classes, one for spring-sown and the other for autumn-sown onions. What exactly is meant by autumn-sown onions? These are usually sown in August, which is summer, or in January and February, which is winter. I have rarely, if ever, known anyone to sow onions in the autumn. So in our local schedule last year we altered this time-honoured description and had three classes. One, spring-sown in the open ground, complete with tops; two, onions sown last year; and three, onions sown this year indoors and transplanted. We found that it answered very well, and caused less argument.

As a rule on new ground, and on old ground, too, if it happens to lack depth, it is difficult to grow good onions, but you can usually manage a crop of shallots, and shallots are very good substitutes for onions, especially the giant type, which often reach a considerable size. Here again is a point for flower show committees. There ought to be two classes for shallots, one for the giants, and one for the small type, which are ideal for pickling. It isn't easy for a dish of perfect little ones to compete with a dish of perfect big ones; they are better kept separate. Shallots are not difficult to grow; they like a good soil, of course, but the main idea is to get it well broken down to get a fine surface, or tilth, for planting. The bulbs are then simply pressed into the soil to about half their depth, or a little more, nine inches apart, in rows a foot apart, and so long as the crows don't pinch them they need very little further attention, apart from keeping the weeds down. There is an old country idea that shallots should be planted on the shortest day and lifted on the longest, but I think it must be another of my old friend, Freddie Grisewood's gardening super-stitions, for I don't think there is anything in it. Planted in February, or as soon as the soil is workable, and harvested in July, seems to produce much better results. Last year many people grew a nice crop of shallots from seed instead of bulbs, because shallot bulbs were scarce, and they most likely will be this year. You can grow very nice shallots from seed, but it's no use planting the bulbs again this year. If you do they will simply run to seed instead of producing a cluster of new bulbs. So if you have saved any you may as well eat them. Actually, they are not true shallots, but a species of onion, and although a very good imitation of the shallot, their natural habit is that of the onion, bulb the first year, seed the second.

February

ABOUT POTATOES

I THINK we might usefully consider the potatoes for a few minutes to-day, because they are probably the most important of all our war-time vegetables. I don't know how many vitamins potatoes contain, but I do know that they have often kept people, as well as pigs, alive during times of famine, and I know that our hens lay more and bigger eggs when they get a daily ration of boiled potatoes, and that's enough to convince me that there must be plenty of food value in them. In fact, I've been told by those who ought to know, that potatoes supply more food per acre than any other crop. So if we all keep a good stock of potatoes in the store and use them sensibly we shall never starve. I said use them sensibly, but a good many people don't do that, and I believe some people don't yet know the real flavour of a good potato. I found it out when I was a small boy; my father used to boil up the little potatoes in an old copper for the pigs and chickens, and many a time have I poked a sharpened stick into the seething cauldron and picked out a nice clean one, peeled off the thin skin, and eaten it like an apple. Ever since then I have preferred potatoes boiled whole, and only the outer thin skin removed after boiling, a bit messy perhaps, and too much trouble for some people, but I honestly think it is the only way to get the full flavour of a good potato, and not only the flavour but the goodness too, because most of the food value is just under the skin—there isn't much except starch and water in the middle—and it seems a great pity to peel off all the best of a potato and throw it away, especially in war-time. I met a man one day with a big bowl of thick potato peelings, and I asked him what he was going to do with them. "Boil 'em for the pig," he said. So I enlarged on the food value, and suggested that if he were to eat the thick peelings and give the insides to the pig it would probably be much better for him. He thought it over for a moment and said, "Then I suppose I should get fat instead of the pig, and what good would that do?" So I let it go at that. After all, I suppose it's no business of mine what you do with your potatoes; my job is to talk about growing them, so let us see if we can get a real bumper crop this year.

In the first place, potatoes like good rich soil to grow in; they have a lot to do in a short time, they are sub-tropical plants, and have to do all their growing and maturing in our comparatively short summer, so we must do all we can to help them. Firstly, by preparing them so that they are all ready from the word go, to get going and keep moving, and secondly, to see that conditions are favourable for good growth. The ideal, if we could give it to them, would be a rich soil, well dug and manured, with plenty of rotten stuff in it, which would keep moist during the first half of the summer while they are growing, gradually drying off in the late summer while they are maturing and getting ready for the harvest. We can't always attain the ideal condition, but we can aim at it. So I suggest that, if you haven't already done it, the potato ground should be dug deeply now, and some good old rotten stuff buried down below. A few handfuls of hop manure, poultry manure, or a good potato fertilizer scattered over the lower spit while you are digging will do a lot of good. But don't give them fresh lime. There's a tremendous lot of lime being thrown about just now, perhaps because its cheap and plentiful, and has had a good boosting. Mark you, I am saying nothing against that; lime is essential in the soil for most vegetable crops, it helps to prepare the other plant foods, but it isn't a substitute for natural manure; you don't give lime *instead* of manure, you give lime to help the soil to digest the manure, and there is no value in excess—too much is merely wasting it. Now potatoes, strangely enough, although they benefit by the after-effects of lime, don't like it fresh, so it is better to miss the potato patch when the lime is being scattered. Some people are under the impression that lime cures the potato scab, it doesn't. If anything, it makes it worse. If potatoes on your ground are inclined to be scabby, one of the best and simplest cures is to dig a nice lot of green grass, lawn mowings for preference, into the soil just before planting. This seems to attract the scab organisms and keep it away from the potatoes. I expect most of you have bought your seed potatoes by this time. I hope so, because the time is getting on. If you haven't, get them as soon as you can, and, if possible, get them from the North-certified stocks. There is no doubt that Scotch or Northern Ireland seed gives better results than those grown in the southern half of England—probably immaturity has something to do with it. Potatoes in Scotland don't get quite so ripe and hard as they do in the south, and they are lifted before they get badly infected with the mysterious virus disease. Then, of course, seed growing in Scotland and Northern Ireland is a specialized industry, and a good deal of care is taken over it. If you had Scotch seed last year and have saved some for planting again, they should be quite satisfactory. Or there is no harm in buying the seed which is known as "once grown." I always think you get a more uniform crop the second year—not so many outsize specimens as you do from new Scotch seed—but that may not apply to all varieties.

When you get your seed potatoes the first thing to do is to sort them over and set them up in trays or boxes for sprouting. If you examine a seed potato you will find most of the eyes at one end, so you should stand them in the trays with this end upwards. Put the trays on a shelf or somewhere where they get all the light possible, but not a very warm place, nor, on the other hand, a very cold place. If they are too warm they soon begin to grow and produce long tender shoots, which are no good, but if they are too cold they won't grow at all, so you should aim at the happy medium, cool, but comfortable. The idea is to induce them to start growing slowly so that by planting time they have some nice sturdy little green shoots on them which are not easily knocked off. This advanced sprouting is a very real advantage, it saves a good deal of time, which is important in the case of potatoes. It's no use planting them early in the cold wet ground; they don't grow any quicker for that. They just wait there, shivering and uncomfortable till the soil gets warmer, and by that time they have caught a nasty cold, and it takes them some time to get going. But if you get them ready sprouted beforehand, and keep them out of the ground till it has felt the influence of the spring sun, then they will grow quickly, without any checks and delays, and very soon walk past those which were planted earlier. I never plant potatoes till the middle of April, unless it may be a few earlies in a sheltered corner, but I make sure that they are nicely sprouted before I plant them. Sprouting also gives you some measure of control over the subsequent crop. A potato planted with all its sprouts intact, that is if most of them grow, will produce a plant with several stems and a large number of small potatoes. On the other hand, if all the sprouts but one are removed, you will get a plant with a single stem and a heavier crop of large potatoes. The new potatoes are produced on stolons which spring from the stems, so assuming that each stem carries six young potatoes, it follows that a plant with five stems would have thirty, and a plant with one stem would have only six, but the plant would put as much energy into the six as it would into the thirty, therefore, the six would be about five times as big as the thirty small ones. It doesn't always work out like this, of course, but you can regulate it to a certain extent. I usually leave two sprouts on each tuber for the main crop, because I like medium to fair-sized potatoes for keeping, but in the case of earlies I leave them all on, because I prefer them small and in large numbers. My experience is that you get a heavier crop from one or two shoots than you do from half a dozen.

I expect the samples of seed potatoes this year will be a bit uneven, with a good many big ones among them, and it is, of course, more economical to cut these big ones in two, because half a potato will often give as good a crop as a whole one, provided there is a good healthy sprout or two at the top. You should always cut a seed potato lengthwise, from top to bottom, not across, because the lower half doesn't give such good results. Then the question arises, when should we cut them, and under what conditions? There is a good deal of controversy about this. Some people maintain that you should cut them well in advance of planting, and put the cut pieces out in the sun and wind to dry. Some of our members had quite a heated argument about it at a recent meeting. No doubt at first sight it does look quite reasonable to dry the cut pieces immediately after cutting, and they are such good-natured things that most of them usually survive if you do. But it doesn't do them any good, and it is much better not to dry them but to keep them on the moist side. I wonder if I can explain this?

To begin with, a potato tuber is not a root, as is often supposed. It is actually part of an underground stem and is in some ways constructed and behaves the same as any other stem. Now if you cut a stem of an ordinary plant, say a geranium cutting for the sake of argument, you wouldn't put it out in the sun to dry, would you? You would keep it moist. A potato, being dormant, is obviously not so dependent on moisture as an active geranium cutting, but the principle is something the same. The first thing that happens is that a corky layer, or callus, grows over the newly cut surface to protect it and seal it up, and this happens much quicker and more successfully in a moist atmosphere than it does in a dry one. So if you decide to cut up your seed potatoes in advance, it is better to choose a wet day for the job, or to cover them afterwards for a time with damp matting or light material of some kind. They will recover from the operation more successfully that way. For my own part I never cut them in advance at all. I cut them as I plant them and put them straight into the ground, and it answers very well. Some people dip them in plaster of paris or powdered lime, it's supposed to prevent bleeding; perhaps it does, but I never bother about that. Don't be in a hurry to plant, you don't gain anything by it. If we could be sure of a perfect spring, free from late frosts or continuous cold rain, early planting might pay, but in nine out of ten of our English springs it doesn't. So I shall have more to say about planting later on. Meantime, get the tubers set out for sprouting, mind they don't get frozen, and above all, give them all the daylight you can, otherwise they will soon be bristling with long white tender shoots which will all get broken off, and then they will have to start at the beginning again.

Finally, just a word about the root crops, parsnips, carrots, beetroots, and so on. You are probably preparing the ground for these as well as for the potatoes, but their requirements are rather different. Whereas the potatoes like a rich diet of plenty of strong manure, the root crops don't like it at all. Perhaps that isn't quite correct. I daresay the root crops like it all right; in strongly manured ground they would grow into big coarse plants, but their roots would be forked and fanged and covered all over with rough whiskers, which doesn't suit our purpose at all. We

want clean straight roots, and to get these we must avoid
an over-rich diet. That doesn't mean that they grow well
in poor soil. The ideal for all these root crops is a deep
well-worked soil which was well treated for the previous
crop, but without fresh muck in it. A little superphosphate
would do it good, and nearly all the root crops respond well
to a dressing of lime.

SEED SUPPLIES

I have just been having a look through some of the new
seed catalogues, and I have had quite a pleasant surprise.
I rather expected to find a large number of blanks in the
lists of popular varieties, and when you consider the difficulties the seed trade must be up against, something of the
kind might well have been expected. In normal times large
quantities of our seeds are grown in other countries,
countries which are now at war with us, and many sources
of supply have completely dried up. In spite of all this, and
the difficulties of staffs and transport, the seed merchants
seem to be delivering the goods almost as usual. It's a
marvel to me how they manage it. True there *are* shortages
of certain kinds and varieties, and you mustn't expect to
make out a list of all your favourites and get them packed
off to you in the good old style, it just can't be done. We
must expect delays and disappointments, we must expect
substitutes; if we can't get the kind we want we must be
satisfied with the nearest to it, and we may have to
rearrange our plans a little and grow something different
to what we had originally intended to. But it is very satisfactory to know that there are enough of the essential
vegetable seeds to go round, and produce all that is really
necessary, provided we use reasonable care. So instead of
grousing let us have a look through a catalogue or two and
see what is going. I notice that among the seeds which are
scarce, and which we are advised to do without, are Golden

Thistles, Calsbresse, Pokeweed, Chinese Cabbage, Jacon, Udo-Oudo, and Winter Purslane. Well, I think we can manage to exist without any of them. I'm sorry to hear that the Seakale Beet, or Swiss Chard, is in short supply, because I consider it a good war-time vegetable, and I have often recommended it. Two of my catalogues offer it as usual, so I take it there is a certain amount available, but you mustn't be disappointed if you can't get it. The same applies to sugar peas, they seem to have disappeared altogether. With regard to ordinary peas I don't think there is much to worry about. Some of the popular varieties are in short supply, but the catalogues still offer a list of about fifty varieties, and if you can't find what you want there you must be hard to please. I have a list here of some sixty varieties of peas: it seems impossible that they can all be different. I suppose they all have their little peculiarities, but I should think some of them must be so much alike that a blind man couldn't tell the difference. The same applies to cabbages. I could take half a dozen popular varieties from different sources and grow them altogether, and I would take on a sporting bet that not one per cent. of you could pick out one from another. I've tried it myself and found it extremely difficult to see any real difference in them. So I suggest that you have a word with your seedsman, and if he hasn't got the one you ask for he will probably have another just as good.

Among the peas which seem to be fairly plentiful are of the round-seeded early varieties, Alaska, Bountiful, and Laxton's Superb. I always used to think Laxton's Superb was an apple, but it seems to be a pea as well, and a very good one too; it grows about two feet high or a little more, and is very early. Of the wrinkled varieties there are plenty to choose from. Gradus, one of the best earlies, seems to be plentiful enough, and so does Lincoln; and if you only had those two you wouldn't do so badly, but there are plenty more. Pilot Foremost and Onward, all varieties which I have often recommended, are not too plentiful, and you may or may not be able to get them. Broad beans seem to be satisfactory, except perhaps the green long-pod variety, which is a bit scarce.

Runner beans may be a bit difficult, they always are after a wet harvest time, and the choice may be limited, but I think we shall get enough if we use them sparingly, and make half a pint go as far as a pint usually goes. If they are properly spaced out very few allotment holders or back-gardeners ever need more than half a pint. Of the beetroots, Detroit and Crimson Globe seem to be fairly plentiful; they are both good varieties which would satisfy most requirements, but there are limited supplies of the other varieties too. The Brassicas appear to be fairly good, but here again you won't be able to pick and choose just as you would like.

There is plenty of broccoli seed, and of the kales, the Tall Green curled, seems to be more plentiful than most of the others. Brussels sprouts should present no great difficulties. Dalkeith and Evesham Giant appear to be in good supply, and most of big seed firms are able to supply their own selected strains. We can still get my two favourite cauliflowers, Snowball and Veitch's Autumn Giant, and I want nothing better. If I had twenty to choose from I should choose Veitch's Autumn Giant as the best cauliflower of the lot, so that's all right.

Carrot seed ought not to be scarce, nor should parsnip seed, as they are both natives. I think there is plenty of parsnip seed, some varieties of carrots are rather short, but there are good supplies of Early Market, Chantenay, Redcored, and Half Long Danuers. Lettuces, radishes, and parsley are in plentiful supply, so we needn't worry about them; most of the popular varieties are available, and there doesn't seem likely to be a shortage of spinach, or spinach beet. I notice, too, that we can get seed of sweet corn, or maize, which is becoming a popular vegetable. The variety, Golden Bantam, is probably the best, and is the only one offered by many of the seedsmen.

Allotment holders don't usually grow their tomatoes from seed; it is usual to leave it to the nurseryman and buy the plants all ready for planting out. If, however, you do prefer to raise them yourselves, there are fair supplies of Sunrise, Kondine Red, and Ailsa Craig, and I don't know that you want anything much better. Turnip seed does not seem to be scarce. Such popular varieties as the Milans, Snowball, White Stone, and Golden Ball are available.

I am glad to see that there is a good supply of late savoy. Ormskirk late green is very plentiful, and I always advocate the growing of a late savoy, so that it follows the brussels sprouts instead of maturing at the same time, so I am not worrying about savoys.

I am told that there is a shortage of vegetable marrow seeds, especially the trailing kinds. I don't quite understand that. I should have thought it was easy enough to save marrow seed, you can get enough from one marrow to supply a couple of dozen allotment holders. I've still got a ripe marrow or two hanging up. I must see what the seed inside them is like. I don't see why it shouldn't be quite sound and good.

Onion and leek seed is going to be a bit difficult; good leek seed is scarce and expensive, and some varieties of onions are very scarce. But there seems to be a good supply of the standard varieties such as Bedfordshire Champion, Up to Date, White Spanish, and the Globes. For my part, if I can get a good strain of Bedfordshire Champion I am quite satisfied.

So you see, what it all boils down to is that the seed trade has risen to the occasion most nobly, and almost like conjurers fetching rabbits out of a hat, they have produced under great difficulties enough of the essential vegetable seeds to supply our legitimate needs. We may not be able to pick and choose, and we may not be able to get all the favourites we have always sworn by, but we shall be able to get others just about as good, and perhaps even a little better. We may not be able to get seeds of some of the less common or novelty vegetables, but we can manage very well without them; they are interesting, but not essential, and so long as we can get supplies of the things that matter, and concentrate more or less on them, we needn't worry about the odds and ends. If we practise sensible economy and avoid waste, and work together as much as possible, we shall have very litte to complain of. When I say work together, I am thinking of local societies or groups, where it should be possible to make an ounce of onion or leek seed go very much further, by getting it sown under glass and distributing the young plants to the members. If each individual sows an ounce or two of seed, and then throws half the plants away at thinning time, or has half a packet of seed left over, somebody may have to go short. But I have laboured this point before, so let it go at that. There is one other point I ought to mention: the varieties of vegetables I have been talking about are the standard varieties, which are usually produced in bulk and distributed through the wholesale trade to the retailers all over the country, and my observations are largely based on reports obtained through the wholesale channels. They take no account of the large retail seed houses whose names and reputations are well known to the gardening world. Most of these firms have their own special strains and varieties, and their own source of supply, which is to a certain extent independent of the wholesale market. It may be, in fact I know it is so, that these firms can still offer seeds of special varieties of vegetables which would be difficult, if not impossible, to obtain elsewhere. So if you have your own favourite seed firm, my advice is, send for their new seed catalogue, and see what they are offering.

You will find a great many varieties which I haven't mentioned, and probably some which I have spoken of as being scarce. So on the face of it, it may look a bit contradictory, because I have had the general supply in mind this afternoon, and not the special stocks in the hands of these well-known retail firms.

For example, I have a new catalogue here which offers six varieties of leeks and nineteen varieties of onions, but that doesn't prove that there is no general shortage of these seeds. It means that this particular firm has its own special stocks of its own special varieties, as well as selected strains of many of the standard varieties. Send for one of these catalogues, and look for yourself. The firms won't send you a catalogue unless you ask for one, so it's up to you. You will find the prices rather high, and you'll grumble about them, and perhaps write to me about it, but I hope you won't. If you knew the years of patience and experience and the amount of work behind these packets of selected strains of seeds you wouldn't think them unduly expensive: and after all, if you get a fine crop of something next summer or autumn, you'll have forgotten by then whether you paid a shilling or one and threepence for the packet of seeds, and you'll have no regrets.

Now one other matter—I have had a letter from the organizers of the Red Cross Agricultural Fund, and they ask me to appeal to all local garden societies to hold their show this year, if possible, in aid of this very deserving cause. Gardeners are always charitable, so if your society has decided to hold a show next summer it would be a nice idea to let the Red Cross benefit by it. If you haven't thought about a show perhaps you'll consider it at your next meeting. You have to make preparations well ahead. You can get a great deal of valuable assistance and advice

on the subject from the Chairman of the Red Cross Horticultural Section, Mr. Walter Brett, whose address is 34
Southampton Street, Strand, London, W.C. 2. So what
about it?

RAKING AND SOWING

If you look through almost any gardening book you are
pretty sure to come across the word tilth, an ancient word
well understood by professional gardeners, but not quite so
clear to the average beginner. What does the word mean?
My dictionary puts it thusly: "Tilth: the operation of
tilling; tillage; husbandry; the state of being tilled." Quite
so! Perfectly clear, isn't it? But to reduce it to common, or,
shall we say garden, English, when we speak of tilth we
usually have in mind the finishing-off process after digging,
reducing the surface of the soil to a fine powdery condition
for the convenience of sowing seeds, and to make life easier
for them, especially during their early infancy. I was talking about this one day to a class of schoolboys when one of
them argued that Nature doesn't prepare a fine tilth for
sowing seeds and yet the wild plants grow and flourish.
Quite true, up to a point, but Dame Nature in wild life
doesn't produce heavy crops of exaggerated carrots and
onions. She has appointed the gardener to be her chief
assistant, and endowed him with the ability to improve on
the wild methods. Nature sows seeds lavishly, one might
almost say recklessly and indiscriminately, but only a small
percentage of them find conditions suitable for growth;
the majority perish. It's a good thing they do, for if every
wild seed grew to a mature plant there wouldn't be room
in the world for them to exist. But in the garden it is a very
different matter, we are dealing with seeds which have
been produced under artificial conditions, seeds which
could not hold their own under the wild laws of nature,

seeds which are too valuable to be cast on stony ground, or otherwise wasted. We want at least the majority of them to grow into healthy plants, so we must make conditions comfortable for them so that none of them perish in the common struggle for existence. Therein lies the art of the gardener, and the importance of the word tilth. During the autumn most of you dug the ground deeply and stocked its larder with plant foods. You left it rough and open so that the frost could penetrate to pulverize and break up the solid lumps. Now the season approaches when we must prepare it for the seeds by breaking down the rough lumps and producing a fine surface. On most soils this can only be done when the weather is dry, and the soil is in a workable condition; if it is wet and sticks all over your boots and clogs up the tools, it is better to keep off it and wait for a more favourable opportunity. There is no desperate hurry, you are not compelled to get certain seeds in by a certain date. Much better to be guided by the weather and the condition of the soil; plodding about on heavy wet soil does it more harm than good and more often delays action than otherwise. The first thing to consider is lime. I am not going to discuss the merits of lime, we have already had a good deal to say on that subject. Your soil may need lime or it may not, that is something I can't tell you, but, assuming that you did everything else in the autumn in the way of digging and manuring, and you have reason to think that lime is necessary, now is the time to apply it. If you are in any doubt about it give everything a dressing except the potato plot, potatoes don't need it. On the rest of the ground it won't do any harm, it is more likely to do good. Spread it over the soil at the rate of half a pound to each square yard, and then lightly fork it in, levelling and breaking up the surface soil as you do so. The final operation takes place a few days before you sow the seeds. First, spread over the soil a sprinkling of

123

superphosphate, at the rate of one ounce to each square yard. Superphosphate has a very real influence on germination. I have proved over and over again that with a little of it in the soil seeds start off very much better than they do without it. An even better plan is to wait till you sow the seeds, then when you put the lime down, sprinkle a little superphosphate along the row before you make the drill with the hoe; this works it into the soil. After all there is no need to have it between the rows, only the weed seeds get the benefit of it there. If superphosphate is difficult to get, steamed bone flour will do just as well. In any case, whether you put it on before or afterwards, give the soil a thorough good raking to get the top inch or two as fine as you can, and rake off all big stones, and anything else that ought not to be there. This fine surface, or tilth, enables the soil to paste round the seeds and keep them moist and cosy, whereas in rough soil some of them roll down the crevices and get lost, and others drop into pockets or vacuums where they get a poor chance of doing anything. Sow all vegetable seeds thinly, not only in the interests of economy, but for the sake of the seedlings themselves. If they come up all jostling each other like a crowd at a football match, they can't possibly do themselves justice, and you have to pull three parts of them out to give the others a chance to breathe. We can't avoid a certain amount of thinning, but the less we have to do the better for the crop. It isn't easy to sow seeds thinly: I know that only too well, especially if you are not used to it, and if you are not careful you will find that an ounce of, say onion seed, has gone into one row, when it ought to have done half a dozen. You want a little practice. Get a packet of seeds now, I daresay you've got some in the cupboard somewhere, dark coloured ones for preference. Clear a few of the plates and things off the table, empty the packet into the palm of your left hand, or the other way round if you happen to be left-handed; then take a few between your thumb and first two fingers, and sow a thin row across the white table-cloth. I'm not suggesting that the table-cloth is in such a condition that they will grow there; this is only practise, and you will pick them up again afterwards. When you've finished try to imagine each of those seeds, or even half of them, growing up into full-sized plants, and you'll soon see that you've sown far too many. Keep on practising till you get the knack of it, and can space them out comfortably. Obviously, however careful you are, you've got to sow more than you need; it wouldn't do to sow onion seeds spaced out at six inches apart, half of them might not come up, so you have to make allowances for failures, but even so, nearly everybody, professional gardeners included, sow far more seeds than they need do. Most of the small seeds are sown in narrow drills or trenches made with a corner of the hoe alongside a line. Good gardeners always use a line to keep the rows straight. Some people seem to think they possess a straight eye and can manage more or less by guesswork, but they usually make a slovenly sort of job of it. I'm rather proud of my lines, I've got four or five; some are just plain to mark out lines for sowing. One has a knot at every six inches, and another has a knot at nine inch intervals. I find these very handy at thinning time or for planting out lettuces, cabbages, or potatoes, it does away with guesswork, saves a lot of measuring, and therefore a lot of time. For instance, suppose you are planting out young onions at six inches apart, or shallots at nine inches apart, you've got a pretty good eye if you can guess the distances correctly. But if you put down your line and plant one opposite each knot you can't very well make a mistake. It may not be necessary to be absolutely exact, but it makes a much neater and smarter job of it if you are. Most of the vegetables are sown in rows a foot apart, to enable you to get between them with a hoe, and when you mark out the rows at sowing time you should make sure that you move both ends each time. Novices sometimes measure off a foot and move the line at one end, and forget to move it at the other; then when your seedlings come up you get a case of parallel lines meeting at the end, and the rest of the rows slightly skew-whiff or, being Sunday, shall we say askew? After sowing, always mark the ends of each row with a stick or label, so that you know where they are. Weeds are often much quicker than cultivated plants, and sometimes the plot is green with weeds before your seedlings are showing. In that case you can put your line along the rows and hoe between them, but not if you've forgotten exactly where they are.

It is early yet for sowing out of doors, but there are a few which can go in before this month is out, always provided the soil is in the right condition. Parsnips are among the first to be sown. They are usually sown in a narrow drill about an inch deep, and when you sow them remember that they will have to be thinned out eventually to nine inches apart. Parsnip seed is very light, something like sowing confetti, so don't choose a windy day, or you may have a job to keep it in the rows. After sowing, rake the soil over the seeds by moving the rake backwards and forwards along the rows, not across them, because that often pulls the seeds out of the line. A deep soil is essential for parsnips so that they can push the big, fat root straight down; if it runs into an obstruction it will turn sideways, or perhaps divide, and send half the root one way and half the other. In shallow, stiff, or stony soils, some gardeners make special deep holes for parsnips with a crowbar, nine inches apart; these holes should be at least six inches across the top, narrowing as they get deeper. The holes are filled up with sifted soil, gently pressed down, and a seed or two sown at the top of each, thinning them to one when they come up. You can grow long carrots in the same way if you like to go to the trouble and want perfect specimens.

Your broad beans can also go in now. Even if you sowed them in the autumn, you might chance another row or two now, just in case. Broad beans are not much appreciated unless you get them early, and by sowing them now you often dodge the black fly, or get less of it. I use a trowel for broad beans. I put down the line marked at every six inches and put a row in each side of it, so that they are in a double row, six inches apart each way. Then a space of about fifteen inches, and another double row. I straddle across the row, carrying the beans in my left-hand pocket, nick out a hole about two inches deep with the point of the trowel, and drop in a bean: it doesn't make any difference which way up they are. At the end of each row I straighten myself and watch the world go round for a moment, and then run the rake over them to finish off the surface. I usually chance a row of round spinach at the end of this month. In the North, or exposed districts, a fortnight later would be better—it all depends on the weather and the soil—you can't garden by dates whether you are in the North or the South. Spinach is pretty hardy, and I usually get the best row of the season from the first sowing at the end of this month; the later sowings often run to seed too quickly. This one doesn't, and the leaves are usually much bigger, and certainly more appreciated: any early vegetables are. I sow spinach thinly in a drill a good two inches wide, and then don't thin it out till the biggest plants are ready. These I pull out, and cut off the roots— not the orthodox method of growing it perhaps, but it answers very well. The only other crop I put in this month is the shallot. To plant shallots you need a nice, fine soft soil so that you can press the bulbs into it to rather more than half their depth, or so that you can just see the tops. The ground should be well loosened with the fork before

127

planting. If you plant them in an inch or two of fine tilth with firm soil below, the quick-growing roots don't penetrate it very easily, and they push the bulbs up out of the soil, and then you have to press them down again. I usually put them nine inches apart in rows a foot apart. There is just one other point, when you are marking out your plot always have the rows running north and south if you possibly can, so that the sun shines on both sides of them. If your rows run east and west one side gets all the sun and the other none, and this makes a big difference with some of the tall-growing vegetables. I know all this is very elementary stuff, but you would be surprised at the number of letters I get about these simple little matters. So I hope you older and more experienced hands will forgive me. After all, it is the novice who is usually more in need of the advice that I am able to give.

WINTER SUPPLIES

It seems a bit early to talk about next winter when we are all looking forward to the spring and summer, but that's the worst of gardening, you've always got to be planning a year ahead, so to-day, while you are still buying packets of seeds, I want to make sure that you don't overlook some of the less interesting but equally important vegetables which keep the pot boiling during the winter and early spring, because that is when we are most likely to be wanting them. It is so easy to get good supplies during the summer and autumn, you are usually giving stuff away then, but when you get round to this time of year it is often quite a different story. Fresh vegetables are getting scarce, and some of us are wishing we had got a bit more green stuff to add a little variety to the daily rations. So let us for the moment take the summer supplies for granted and think of next winter.

I have already dealt with onions, leeks, and potatoes, so we will take them for granted too. Next in importance comes the Brassica group, or in plain or garden English, the cabbage tribe. There's a lot to be said for a good cabbage, especially when you haven't got one, and they are being sold by the pound in the shops. Cabbage isn't everybody's fancy, of course, and there are a good many people, I believe, who can't digest it, although they may not have found it out yet. An old friend of mine, who is a great gardening authority, never grows cabbage and never eats it, says it's only fit for a cow with a cast-iron stomach, but I believe the majority of us like it and are able to digest it, and even benefit by it. The trouble is that a cabbage is so rarely cooked properly, the usual practice being to boil all the goodness out and throw it away, and eat the mess that's left. There are better ways of cooking it than that. The ladies of my household have been making me drink cabbage water lately as a cocktail before dinner. I didn't like it at first, until I discovered that a few drops of a well-known brand of sauce made it quite palatable—even now I would rather have a gin-and-it, but I find the cabbage cocktail quite tolerable, and it produces such an appetite that you hardly notice what you are eating afterwards, which is sometimes a good thing.

However, I won't say much about growing cabbages, no doubt you've all got a bed of spring cabbages coming along, and you will be sowing or planting a few of one of the summer and autumn varieties such as Winningstadt. The one I would like to recommend is the little hardy colewort, just a small packet of seed, while there is some to be had, but don't sow it till May or even June. This is a sweet, hard-hearted little cabbage which doesn't take up much room and lasts into the winter, and often comes in very handy.

Another type of cabbage which we don't always make

the best of is the savoy, because it so often turns in when there are plenty of sprouts and we don't appreciate it. I suggest that you get a small packet of an early variety for sowing in March, and using before you start on the brussels sprouts, and a packet of a late variety to sow in May, and use after the brussels are finished. A good late savoy is often very acceptable.

My own favourite of all the Brassicas is the brussels sprout. I could eat them every day through the winter without getting tired of them. It's a good job we are not all alike, but I believe most people like sprouts, and you are not likely to overlook them, so I needn't say much about them, except that I think it pays to sow them early, at least some of them. I like to make two sowings of brussels, one early in March and the other in April, the idea being to spread over the supply from early November till the end of February if possible. It doesn't always come off, but there's no harm in trying, and I would always rather sow them in boxes in a cold frame than out of doors.

This applies to all the Brassicas which are sown in the spring. I am not saying that it is necessary, it isn't, but it does give you more control over them, you can protect them from the birds easier, and you can give them nice, finely-sifted soil for germination. Of course, you have to transplant them to the seed bed before they get over-crowded in the boxes. This means a little more trouble, but it is a distinct advantage, because it keeps them on the move, and that is what Brassicas like, to keep steadily growing right from the start without coming to a stand-still through being crowded together waiting for the next move. You may say, "All very well," but you can't afford a cold frame. Well, you ought to see some of mine. Four bits of board with a pane of glass, or even only a bit of old fish-netting over the top. I ought to be thoroughly ashamed of them, but they answer very well, so why worry?

I find one of the commonest troubles with brussels and autumn cauliflowers is that the plants are ready for putting out long before the ground can be prepared for them, because there is another crop on it, and most people wait till the summer crops are cleared before planting out the greens. That, of course, is much more convenient, but if you space out your early peas, carrots, and other early crops with this in view, you can plant the brussels and cauliflowers between them as early as May and June. There won't be serious overcrowding, because the early crops will be cleared before the greens have grown very big.

The broccoli is another very acceptable winter vegetable, but a bit tricky for beginners; it needs experience as well as a favourable season to get a good bed of late broccoli, and the late varieties are much more valuable than the early ones. The exception is the purple sprouting variety. I should advise everybody to plant out a row or two of these. You needn't sow them or plant them out quite so early as the brussels. If you can plant them after the early potatoes have been lifted it will do nicely. They will stand through the winter and then, just when you are in need of something in the spring, the purple shoots will appear and provide a very appetising dish. I have only one fault to find with them, they sometimes sprout out altogether and get past their best before you can use them, but we have to chance that.

I suppose that kales would usually find themselves at the bottom of the list as far as popularity goes. They ought to be somewhere near the top, because, although they may not compare in flavour or quality with brussels sprouts or cauliflowers, they turn in for use long after the others are finished, and just when we want them. There are several types of kale to choose from, some of them as handsome as a fern, and others with several colours in the leaves and beautiful enough for the flower border. But from the kitchen point of view, I personally prefer the cottagers' or sprouting kinds. These grow something like a brussels sprout, only instead of solid round sprouts they produce young shoots, which you pick off and cook in the usual way, and if you catch them just right the flavour is very good indeed, and, as I said before, they come in the spring when there is precious little else to be had.

Nearly all the Brassicas are very good-natured things as regards soil and climate; the main requirements are firm soil with plenty of lime in it. They all come from one common ancestor, a wild Brassica which usually grows in solid chalk. There is one other that I might have mentioned, the red cabbage, usually grown for pickling but quite good if cooked in the ordinary way, and one of the easiest of all to grow.

Personally, I like pickled cabbage cooked, and if I had my way I should have several large jars pickled every year, and then I should have it cooked during the winter, especially when I had pork. You try it, if you ever get any pork, and see if you don't agree with me. I was in the dining-room of a hotel once, and at the next table was a large German woman. She started her meal by emptying a jar of pickled cabbage into a soup plate and eating the lot—the noise she made scrumping it was something terrific—and when she had finished it she drank the vinegar. Perhaps it was the nearest thing she could get to sauerkraut, and she seemed much better for it, but somehow I've never been able to enjoy raw pickled cabbage since—so I have it boiled.

All the big Brassicas, that is, brussels, kales, cauliflowers, and broccoli, should be planted two feet apart each way, you don't gain anything by crowding them. Cabbages can be put a little closer, say eighteen inches. With a little manœuvring and selection you can maintain a constant supply of Brassicas in one form or another all round the year, and that, I think, is what we should aim at this year, because they add that little something to the diet that the others haven't got.

Have you ever heard of anyone storing cabbages in a clamp? Perhaps not, and I shouldn't think it has often been attempted. But a friend of mine had a lot of good solid cabbages; he couldn't sell them, nobody wanted them, and he didn't keep goats or rabbits, but he wanted the ground, so he cut the cabbages, stacked them in a heap against a wall, and covered them with straw. And there they remained for a month or two until they began to stink and he had to do something about it. When they were uncovered they rather resembled a muck heap, in more ways than one, and he decided to use them as such. However, we discovered that they were still solid, although brown and rotten-looking, but when we peeled off the outer dead layer of leaves, there, lo and behold, were solid white hearts, as crisp and fresh as anything you could wish for. It was mainly the outer loose leaves that had gone bad, the hearts were almost perfect and excellent flavour. Most of them were bought by a greengrocer and the others lasted practically through the winter, hardly any of them were wasted. Whether it would always happen like that I can't say, but it proved that cabbages *can* be stored, and it might be worth trying when there is a glut about. I have sometimes kept cauliflowers in good condition for a fortnight by pulling them up and hanging them upside down along the north side of the shed. It often happens that cauliflowers or brussels are all ready together, or more than can be used, so if you can spread them over even a fortnight it is worth doing.

Now what of the other good winter vegetables—celery, for instance? Celery, strangely enough, doesn't seem to carry much weight in official schemes. The food experts don't seem to say much about it. Perhaps its food value isn't very high, or it may not contain enough vitamins and things. I can easily understand that, because the wild celery is a poisonous narcotic and grows in filthy swamps, but the cultivated brand is very wholesome and palatable. Some people say it cures or prevents rheumatism. Certainly I eat celery and I don't get rheumatism yet, so there must be something in it. Of course, we must think of the food value of our war-time vegetables, it ought to be the first consideration, but not necessarily the only one. If we get too faddy about it we shall make ourselves miserable and imagine all sorts of things, and, after all, a little of what you fancy does you good, and I, for one, often fancy a little celery now and then, either cooked or raw. Celery is a peculiar vegetable, tender in its infancy, but hardy in its old age. It requires a long season of growth, and the seed is usually sown under glass early in the spring. If you have no such convenience I suggest, for a small garden or allotment, that you don't trouble to sow seed, but beg or buy a few plants at planting time. It is too early to talk about celery trenches, but in making your plans reserve a bit of the wettest part of the garden for the celery trench, or, if that is impossible, put it as near to the water supply as possible, so that you won't have so far to carry it. Celery likes water.

You have already made provision for the root crops, such as parsnips, swedes, artichokes, carrots, and beet. In case you haven't, don't overlook them when making your plans. Always keep in mind the winter store, for that is when we are likely to need the food; we are not likely to go short during the summer.

March

PLANT TONICS

Now that the season of sowing and planting is with us, and we are putting the final touches to the ground, we shall naturally be thinking of fertilizers, and I'm afraid these are going to prove something of a problem this year, owing to a shortage of some of the essential plant foods, so we shall have to be careful that we don't get a badly balanced diet, or we may do more harm than good. Let us face the facts; fertilizers in powder form cannot be a complete substitute for farmyard or other natural bulky manures, because, although they supply all the chemical elements necessary, they don't supply the bulky material which forms humus in the soil, and keeps it in a healthy, fertile condition. To use nothing but fertilizers in the garden year after year is rather like trying to live on tonics and tablets, which, although excellent in themselves, cannot take the place of solid food, or not for long, at any rate. We must always remember that manuring the ground means something more than just feeding it; it means keeping the soil healthy, so that it can digest the plant food stored up in it. Don't think I am trying to turn you away from the use of artificial fertilizers, far from it. I wouldn't be without them for anything, and I don't see how we could manage without them, unless we could all get plentiful supplies of good farmyard stuff, which we can't.

All I want you to do is to understand them, and get the best out of them, because they are rather like medicine, used properly, and in the correct quantities, they can do a lot of good, but used carelessly they can just as easily do harm.

Why do I and others always recommend farmyard stuff if you can get it? Simply because it usually contains the essential chemical plant foods in a readily available form, and also the necessary bulky material which decays slowly and releases these foods gradually as they are required. It also keeps the soil stocked with humus, keeps it warm, and helps it to hold moisture during the dry weather. We must always remember that our methods of gardening are not quite natural, and take more out of the soil than it can afford to lose. Obviously you can't take a cart-load of vegetables from a plot, and expect it to go on cropping at the same rate, unless you replenish its losses, and restock it with plant food. The ideal to aim at, if we could do it, would be to return to the soil the equivalent of what we have taken from it, not merely in the chemical sense, but in bulk also. If you take a cart-load of vegetables from the plot and put back a cart-load of farmyard muck, you will have made a fair exchange, the soil will be quite satisfied and produce another cart-load of vegetables.

But if you think you can pay the soil for that load of vegetables with a few handfuls of powder, you will soon find that it soon fails to deliver the goods. Now let us assume that we can't get the farmyard stuff, and rule it out altogether, what are we going to do about it? Take the bulky part first, in farmyard manure this is largely made up of straw, rotten vegetation, and similar material, in various stages of decay. This forms the essential humus in the soil, and it shouldn't be difficult to find a substitute. Any old leaves, waste vegetable matter, household waste which is not fit for food, straw, grass, or anything which has once lived, will rot down into valuable plant food. That is why we have heard so much about the compost heap since the war began, because it takes the place of the bulky part of the farm stuff.

What is a compost heap? I suppose the word compost sounds better than refuse, or rubbish, but that is what it really amounts to.

It is merely a valuable accumulation of waste garden

material which might otherwise be burned, and now is a very good time to start such a heap. Or it needn't be an unsightly heap, a pit is better; or you can make a large bin with four pieces of tin and a few strong stakes. But if you can go to the extra trouble of digging a good big square pit in a corner of the garden, and lining it with concrete, or banging it down well so that the moisture doesn't drain out of it, you will have the ideal collecting place for next year's manure supply. It's surprising what a lot of stuff you can keep throwing into this pit. All your lawn mowings, weeds, hedge and ditch trimmings, old tea leaves and coffee grounds, anything which has no other use. What with the salvage collection, waste food for pigs, and the compost pit, there ought to be nothing left nowadays for the dustman to take away, except bits of broken glass and crockery and coal ashes; these are no use on the compost heap. But nearly everything else is.

I got into trouble recently for including old socks and undies in the waste material, but when I said it, I didn't mean anything that could possibly be made other use of. I had just been poking about in an old damp barn with an earth floor, and I found a heap of what had once been old sacks or mats or something and some ancient garments which were so far gone that you couldn't recognize what they were; they dropped to pieces as you touched them. So I got a fork and dumped the lot on to the compost heap. Obviously you wouldn't put old woollen things there if they were of any possible use as salvage. I often think we take a good deal more away from the vegetable plot than we need to do. Carrot and beet tops, the outer leaves of cabbages, and all that sort of thing. If you give a friend a bunch of beetroots, or sell them, complete with the tops just as you pull them up, you also give away valuable potash as well as bulky material which ought to be kept in your own garden.

I think we ought to make it a practice this year to do all the trimming on the plot, and not to take away anything which is not going to be eaten. Put everything else on the compost. If you keep chickens, throw all the cleanings from the poultry house, straw and all on the heap, or into the pit, and as you do so, sprinkle it lightly with sulphate of ammonia, or one of the advertised preparations for accelerating decay. If you put dry stuff on during the summer, sprinkle it with water as well. You will be surprised how quickly this stuff accumulates, and what a fine stack will be there ready for the autumn digging.

So much for the bulk; now to bring the quality of this compost up to that of farmyard stuff, certain chemical foods must be added to it. This is where the chemical fertilizers come in, and it is not going to be too easy, because some of the essential elements are very difficult to get, but for the sake of interest we all ought to know something of them and what they do. Plants require a considerable number of chemical substances to keep them properly fed; some of them in very small quantities, it is true, but without those small quantities they can't thrive any more than we can without vitamins.

However, fortunately for us, most of them are usually in plentiful supply in the soil, and we don't have to bother about them. If we had to keep them all supplied, plant foods would present a complicated problem.

The three elements which do get used up, and have to be replenished, are potash, nitrogen, and phosphoric acid, or phosphates. These three are absolutely essential, but their functions are quite distinct. Nitrogen is the element which makes plants grow; it produces new leaves, shoots, and soft tender growth, we might call it the growing element. Potash supplies colours, flavours, qualities, and does all sorts of other complicated things, while phosphates build up the hard skeleton parts of a plant, the woody parts, produce maturity, and have a direct effect on the production of seeds, and the ripening and harvesting of a plant. They also assist root action during the early life of a plant.

So you see, one of these alone is not much good, and it doesn't follow that because you get something in a tin or bag called a fertilizer that it is going to make everything in the garden look lovely. It may easily do more harm than good if you use too much of it without some of the others to balance it. Suppose, for instance, that you used only nitrogen, the result would be rapid soft growth, but without any strength or backbone, and the plant would topple over and never reach maturity.

On the other hand, if you had nothing but phosphates, the plants would become hard and stunted and never grow up at all. What we want is a correct balance of these elements, just enough of each, but not too much of any, which is not so easy as it may sound because we never quite know how much of any one of them may already be in the soil. The one which is going to be difficult this year is potash, which is very scarce, so there is not much point in giving you recipes, like we did in the good old days, to mix so much sulphate of potash and so much of the other elements to make the perfect fertilizer, because, although you may get the other two, you probably won't get the potash. The usual suppliers of potash are sulphate of potash and muriate of potash, or potash salts; and if you've got a little of either of them, don't waste it, spread it over the vegetable ground as soon as you like, it doesn't evaporate or waste, but remains in the soil till the plants use it. Other supplies of potash are wood ashes, or the ashes of rubbish fires or anything except coal. Some of these ashes contain an appreciable amount of potash, but it soon gets washed down if you leave them out in the weather, so the best plan is to spread the ashes over the soil where the potash is wanted while they are still fresh and dry. Soot contains a little potash, more, I believe, than some people think, at any rate it produces the same effect. The crops which need the most potash are the root crops, such as carrots and beet, especially beet, and the leaves of beet or marigolds often contain a fair amount of potash, that is why I said never throw away, make sure that they get back into the soil again. We shall need every scrap of potash we can get, and in any form we can get it. The other elements are easier, you can get sulphate of ammonia, which supplies nitrogen, and the danger is that you might get too much, and overbalance it a bit.

If you work it out at 1 lb. per square rod, or half an ounce to each square yard, that is enough as a spring dressing at sowing or planting time. You can give a little more later on, as a tonic to growing plants, but you can easily overdo it, so never give more than a very light sprinkling. Sulphate of ammonia acts quickly, and it is no use putting it in a month or two before planting or it may have disappeared before the plants are there to use it.

Potash and phosphates can be applied at any time, they remain in the soil till used up, but nitrogen is different, and the best time to use sulphate of ammonia is when the crops are actually there and can make use of it. Nitrogen is also supplied by nitrate of soda, nitro chalk, and cyanamide, as well as in such organic fertilizers as dried blood, fish manures, and poultry manures. Some of these supply other good things as well, especially fish manure, and are well worth having if you can get them. Phosphates are supplied in various ways, the two most convenient are bone meal and superphosphate. Basic slag is also a good phosphate, but I expect the farmers will want most of that. Superphosphate is as good as any, and you can apply it now, at the rate of 3 lbs. to each square rod, or $1\frac{1}{2}$ ounces to each square yard, and you should not need any more during the season. It has an excellent effect on germinating seeds, and helps them along quickly. In normal times I might suggest a mixture of these three elements, but there isn't much point in that if you can't get them, so under present circumstances I suggest that you get a ready-mixed or general fertilizer, or a fertilizer made specially for a particular crop, such as potato fertilizer or tomato fertilizer; these are blended to meet the requirements of the crop, and the makers can get the ingredients when we can't. If you go to a reputable firm, you won't go far wrong, because all fertilizers are under Government control. You usually get directions for use on tins or packets; follow them carefully, and don't be tempted to use a bit extra for luck.

TRIALS AND TROUBLES

The crocuses will soon be out, the birds are singing, and this is the time when the gardening fever spreads. Already I notice seed packets are blowing about the allotments instead of into the salvage bin, and take it all round, the garden is full of interest just now. It's nice to think that each little seed we sow is going to grow into a fine carrot or onion as the case may be. But is it? There are a good many little snags and obstacles to be got over before we reach that happy state, and it's just as well to be prepared for them and act accordingly. It doesn't seem to matter what we try to grow, there is always an enemy of some kind waiting to pounce on it and spoil the good work; what with the invading army of birds, cats, moles, insects, and diseases of various kinds, it's a wonder we are able to grow anything at all. But there is one thing we should remember: nearly all these garden troubles can be prevented, but many of them are extremely difficult to deal with once they are allowed to get going. It isn't difficult to settle the first pair of greenflies which hatch out in the spring, but it is quite a different story if we wait till they have bred a family of about a million, and spread them all over the crop. Unfortunately, that is just what many of us do, we forget all about them until the garden is absolutely running alive, and then get panicky, rush about in a frenzy, buy tins of whatever we can get, and squirt it all over the garden in a vain attempt to save our precious crops. Never was the old saying, "Prevention is better than cure," more true than it is in the garden. So we must be forewarned this year, and take timely measures to keep the crops clean. We can't afford to share them with insects in war-time. Let us consider a few of the most formidable of them and see what can be done about them. Just now we are doing a good deal of late digging, to make up for time lost during frosty weather. So while we are turning over the soil we should keep an eye open for any insects which may show themselves. There are a good many enemies in the soil, but there are also good friends, so we must learn to distinguish between the good and the bad, and not slaughter every living thing indiscriminately. A rough guide, and a very useful one, is this: insects which are active and can run about are friends, and should be left alone; they are usually hunters, preying on other insects. The centipede and the long black beetle are good examples of this. This test only applies now, and doesn't include such things as earwigs and woodlice, which don't appear till later in the year. On the other hand, insects which remain more or less in one place and cannot run are nearly always enemies, and must be treated as such. These include wireworms, slugs, and various other sluggish little creatures. Wireworms can be very troublesome, and are usually most abundant in newly broken pasture land, because their natural home is in the turf. Most of you know a wireworm when you see it, but for the benefit of beginners I would describe it as a small yellow grub, about half an inch long, without legs, rather thin, and very tough and wiry. It lives on the roots of most vegetables, and can be very destructive, and it is very difficult to deal with. Catching them and pulling them in half is a fairly effective method, but a rather tedious one, and as they are not very conspicuous you don't easily spot them.

Burying the turf deeply is a useful preventive, they will usually stop in it for the first season. Starlings and other birds are very fond of them, and constant cultivation with the fork and rake and hoe exposes them to the birds. Trapping is another method. Bits of carrots stuck on the end of sticks and buried six inches deep among the plants will attract large numbers; they can be taken out occasionally for examination. I used to trap them by sowing a row of wheat across the plot here and there; wireworms are very fond of wheat and will go to it in preference to most things, and if you dig it up carefully when it's six or seven inches high you often find scores of them among the roots, but I don't know whether we should be allowed to use wheat for that purpose now, even a handful or two. Wireworms are not usually so troublesome in older cultivated soil. They are the grubs of a little grass beetle, and eventually they become beetles themselves. Then they return to the grass, the beetles don't stop long on open soil, so constant cultivation plus trapping is the best remedy. I don't know of any chemical substance that will kill them, or at least, nothing that you could use on the garden. Naphthalene and the advertised soil fumigants are very distasteful to wireworms and often drive them away. A sprinkling of powdered or "whizzed" naphthalene over the soil while digging certainly keeps a good many pests away, and is well worth while, about three ounces to a square yard is enough. Another soil insect, which is prevalent in some districts, but rarely seen in others, is the grub of the cockchafer, or May bug. This is a big white insect, about the size of a shrimp, curled up in the soil; in some parts of the country they call it "Joe Basset," and if you get it in a garden in large numbers you soon find it difficult to grow anything, and wonder what is killing your plants and chewing the roots off. It is fairly easy to see while you are digging, so if you do see one make sure that you put it out of action. Most people put it in a matchbox and send it to me, and it's sometimes rather high when I get it. I received a couple in a little wedding-cake box recently, which was rather disappointing, especially as they were considerably more than dead.

Slugs will soon be making their appearance, and you all know what slugs can do. But, candidly, I never worry about them; I find that a tin of one of the metaldehyde slug destroyers keeps them within harmless limits. You merely put a pinch here and there among the seedlings, and the slugs soon get the tummy-ache and disappear. Of the pests that do their dirty work above ground, perhaps the various flies are the most unpopular. The onion fly, the carrot fly, the parsnip fly, and the celery fly, are all rather similar in their actions. The flies lay eggs at the base of the young plants, the maggots hatch out and get into the roots and the damage is done. In the case of parsnips and celery they lay their eggs on the leaves instead of the roots, and the maggots tunnel into the tissue of the leaf. The only thing then is to squash them with your fingers and thumb, a rather tedious and unpleasant job, so it is much better to try to keep them away and prevent the eggs being laid. In the case of the onion fly, you can often avoid it by sowing seed under glass and planting the seedlings out when they are three or four inches long. The fly doesn't seem to worry about them at that stage, she prefers them very young. If you must sow them out of doors, the best preventive is calomel dust; this should be blown or dusted over the rows as soon as the onions are through the soil, and repeated two or three times during the first month. Some people dust them with soot and lime, or spray over them with a mild paraffin emulsion. Others sow parsley among the onions, the idea being to make them smell nasty to the fly, who finds the crop by sense of smell rather than sight. In the case of parsnip and celery fly, if you can gather leaves from elder trees, crush them and scatter them along the rows, the flies will usually keep away from the objectionable smell of the leaves, and lay their eggs on somebody else's celery. What the onion and carrot fly like are the ragged little holes left at thinning time, which more or less expose the roots of the plants left behind. The disturbing of the plants, too, gives off their pungent smell and attracts the fly to them. I find I can get better crops of both onions and early carrots by sowing the seed very thinly in rather wide drills, and then leaving them undisturbed without any more thinning. You don't get big prize onions that way, but I don't know that you want them this year. A good crop of smaller ones is likely to be more useful. The long carrots for winter use have to be thinned of course, but I never sow them till early June, and by that time the fly has gone, so we don't have to worry about it.

One thing I would advise you to do is to lay in a stock of derris powder, or derris insecticide, while you can get it. You never know, it may get as scarce and difficult as some of the other things, and it is very useful for dusting or spraying the blackfly of the broad beans, and other insects during the summer. It is very useful for dusting the young turnips and Brassica seedlings to keep away the wretched little flea beetle, which riddles the leaves with holes and often destroys the crop before it has a chance to grow up. This pest is most destructive in dry weather when the plants come to a standstill, then he just eats them up. But in a garden we can do a good deal to prevent this by giving the plants a light dressing of sulphate of ammonia or dried

145

blood, and a good watering. This doesn't kill the beetle, but it keeps the plants growing quickly, so that even if the beetle has a nibble at the leaves it doesn't matter much, because new ones grow faster than he can eat them. A dusting of derris powder, however, will usually put a stop to his little tricks.

I suppose the trouble I hear more about than any other is the club root disease of the cabbage, or Brassica family. In certain districts, and on certain types of soil, this disease is probably the most serious trouble the allotment holder has to contend with. It is caused by a slime fungus in the soil, which gets into the roots of the plants during the growing season, causing the cripplings and swellings which a good many gardeners know only too well, and it often means that the plants turn yellow, wilt and die, just when they ought to be approaching maturity. The Brassicas are natives of the chalky or alkaline soils, or at least their ancestors were, and so long as they remain there they don't get the club root disease, because it can only thrive in acid soils, and it is when we grow the cabbage family on the wrong kind of soil that it falls a victim to the disease. The remedy is to try to convert the soil from an acid condition to an alkaline condition, not a particularly rapid process, but a fairly easy one, given the necessary time. Repeated dressings of lime will do it, and the finer the lime the quicker its action. But it's no use trying to hurry it, the best plan is to use hydrated lime, at the rate of 1 lb. to each square yard, or 28 lbs. to each square rod, spread it over the soil and lightly fork or rake it in about a week before planting out. You may not see much difference the first year, but keep repeating it each time you plant, and in three or four years the club should have died out, it depends how bad it is. You needn't keep Brassicas off the ground during treatment, you will usually find that the disease gradually decreases if you stick to the liming.

Of course, all the troubles of the garden are not due to insects or disease. Some of the bigger creatures can also be very destructive. Birds, for instance, are very fond of seeds and seedlings, which must be protected, if necessary, either by proper wire guards or netting, or by stretching strands of black thread along the rows about nine inches from the ground. I haven't much faith in festoons of rags and paper; the birds know what they are there for, besides the salvage people want them. Scarecrows are not much good either. I saw a bird build a nest in one some years ago, and I've never had much faith in them since. I daresay most of you can devise some method of keeping the birds away without hurting them. I don't like hurting birds. I'm afraid I'm not so squeamish about other people's cats and dogs; they can be, and often are, a perfect nuisance on allotments in industrial areas. Cats are difficult, but a lot can be done with a well-aimed lump of dirt. Dogs are inexcusable, and their owners might at least keep them off allotments, even if they themselves are not interested in growing food. Children, too, are sometimes very troublesome, but it's no use blaming them, but those responsible for them might surely exercise a little more control over them where allotments are concerned, for these allotments are a vital source of food supply. Our allotments have recently been visited by a herd of cows. I don't know quite what we can do about them, I know what I felt like doing, but perhaps the less said about that the better, except that I should like to appeal to everybody who owns animals of any kind to do their best to keep them under control, and respect the efforts of those who are trying to increase the food supply.

PRUNING THE ROSES

We haven't had much to say about the flowers lately. Obviously, in these times when food growing is all important, flowers must take a back seat, but it doesn't follow that we must neglect them altogether. If they have all been swept away to make room for more vegetables, then there is nothing more to be said about them, but if they are still there, occupying space, they might just as well be looked after and made the most of. An untidy, neglected flower border, overgrown with weeds and rubbish is neither use nor ornament, and takes up just as much room as a well-kept one. Particularly does this apply to rock gardens and roses; if you've got a little rockery, you might just as well keep it tidy and colourful, and if you've got a few rose bushes, you might just as well look after them and prune them and get a few nice cheerful flowers for the summer. So this afternoon I want to say a few words about pruning roses, because now is the time to do it. If you read some of the rose books, or listen to some of the experts, you can easily get the impression that rose pruning is a complicated and deeply involved business, only to be undertaken by those of long experience and careful training. Actually, it isn't like that at all, it's really a comparatively simple matter, and merely requires a little common sense and a good deal of courage. Let us just consider how a rose bush grows. Every spring it starts at the beginning, as it were, producing entirely new shoots, and these bear the roses during the summer. Some shrubs produce the new shoots during one summer and flowers on them in the next; but the rose doesn't, it does the whole job in the one season, so what we actually do is to cut down the old bush each year, and let it start at the beginning again and grow into a new one. Let us examine an ordinary rose bush at the present time, one which hasn't been pruned, of course. We shall find a number of old branches which grew last year, and carried the flowers. Trace one of these branches down; at the top it may be divided into several thin twiggy shoots, perhaps with last year's seed pods still hanging on them, but lower down it becomes just a single stem and you come to the point where it joins the old part of the bush, somewhere down towards the ground. That is where it started from last year. Now if you look closely, you will find all the way up this stem a number of dormant buds, or eyes, each of which is capable, under favourable circumstances, of growing out into a new shoot; perhaps some of those at the top are already doing so. As a rule, it is the highest buds, those farthest away from the roots, which break out first in the spring, while the lower ones remain dormant, and those high ones, on the thin twigs, are the weak ones, and produce only small shoots and roses. So if you leave the bush as it is, you will most likely get a very untidy tall bush, with small shoots and flowers at the top, and a good deal of dormant bare wood down below, because, so long as the top buds are allowed to grow, those on the lower part of the stem will remain dormant. This doesn't suit our purpose, because these lower buds are capable of producing the strongest shoots and finest roses, especially if we limit their numbers, so that the energy which would otherwise go into a dozen small shoots at the top is concentrated in two or three of these strong lower ones. So we cut off nearly the whole of the present branch, leaving only a piece about as long as your finger at the bottom of each. The buds on this stump will then grow into strong shoots with good flowers, and the bush will remain dwarf and shapely instead of straggly and untidy. Opinions differ as to how long a piece should be left when cutting back last year's branches. Some say leave three buds, others say six, or even nine; the theory apparently being that if you leave six buds you will get six new shoots, and so on. Actually, you can't work it out on mathematical lines like that. If you leave six buds, it doesn't follow that they will all break. Much more likely two or three at the top will break out and the others remain dormant, and the more buds you leave the more bare stem you are likely to get. So my advice is, don't trouble to count buds, but leave a stump about three inches long in each case, always cutting just above a bud which points away from the centre of the bush. When you have finished, all that will be left of your bush, if it has been properly pruned previously, will be a little group of stumps sticking above the ground, something like the fingers on your hand. It requires courage to do it, but it is the only way to get good roses on shapely bushes. Obviously a strong thick stem is capable of carrying more and better shoots than a thin weak one, so you should make it a general rule to cut a weak one lower down than a strong one. Very thin twigs and dead snags should be cut out altogether.

Some varieties of roses are a bit awkward, and refuse to grow in the orthodox manner. Instead, they may send up a great strong shoot as much as six feet high, bearing a number of fine roses. What are you going to do with a shoot like that? If you cut it right down you will probably get another just like it. So a better plan, in this case, is to cut about a foot off the top, then bend the shoot down more or less horizontally, and tie the end to a peg; then the buds all the way along it will break into growth and produce a large number of fine roses without spoiling the level of the bed. So much for ordinary bush roses.

Standards are pruned on the same principle, except that instead of cutting them down to the ground, you cut back last year's shoots fairly close to the head at the top of the main stem. The climbing forms of the Hybrid Teas, such as climbing Madam Butterfly, climbing General Mac-Arthur, and so on, are also pruned now, but they can easily be over-pruned. They are really climbing counterparts of their dwarf namesakes, and usually consist of a number of long canes or branches with side shoots along them. You mustn't be too drastic with them, or they may revert to the dwarf habit and refuse to climb. The best way is to cut about a foot or so off the end of each long cane, and shorten the side shoots to about half their length. If you planted some new ones during the winter, cut out the weak twiggy shoots, but leave the main ones nearly full length, cutting off only about a foot. The line ramblers, such as American Pillar, and Dorothy Perkins, were pruned in the autumn, or should have been, by cutting out the old flowering branches, and leaving the long green ones which grew last summer. It may be that the frost has cut back the ends of these a bit; if so, cut them off well below the damage. Even if there is no damage, it is just as well to cut a little off the ends, it encourages stronger side shoots below, which will carry this year's flowers. The dwarf polyanthus, and hybrid polyanthus, which include the Poulsen varieties, are very popular for beds and borders nowadays, not only because they are easy to grow, but because they keep on flowering right through the summer and autumn. They can also be pruned now; not so drastically as the hybrid teas, indeed some people never prune them at all beyond cutting off the old dead flowers; but I am convinced that a light annual pruning gives much better results. The dwarf types can be cut back, just above a bud about nine inches from the ground; the taller Poulsen types can be left as high as eighteen inches. In any case, it definitely pays to cut them back a little, the resultant growth which breaks out from below the cut gives much finer flowers, and keeps the bushes more shapely and better looking. It is also advisable to thin out the weak twiggy stems, and concentrate only on the strong ones.

It hasn't been much of a season for planting roses, or anything else for that matter, but there is still time, if you want to put in a few new ones. If I were planting new roses as late as this, I should prune them before planting, it's much easier, and less dangerous, especially if you use a knife. You can sit on a box and prune them in comfort. I said if you use a knife—rather an interesting point that.

Most of the professional gardeners and nurserymen always prune with a knife, they would scorn to use secateurs, and maintain that a pruning-knife makes a much cleaner cut, and so it does in the hands of those who know how to use it, but in the hands of an amateur it can become a rather dangerous weapon; it soon raises a blister on soft hands, and if you're not careful, you soon find yourself pulling the bushes out by the roots instead of pruning them, to say nothing of scratching your hands and tearing your clothes. So if you are not used to a knife, take my tip and use a good sharp pair of secateurs, you'll find them much easier. It's true that some of the old-fashioned secateurs made a very clumsy cut, but the modern types are much better, and cut off a stem as clearly and neatly as a knife. Another good shrub which is found in many gardens, and ought to be pruned now, is the purple Buddlea, which is often neglected and allowed to get wild and untidy. Its habit of growth is something like that of the rose; it produces long branches during the spring which bear the purple flower spikes later in the summer. At the present time last year's branches and the dead flowers are probably still there. If you trace them back to their beginning, you will find little tufts of green leaves along the main stems. Cut them right back, leaving only two or three of these tufts at the base of each branch, and from these new branches will grow out and produce large flower heads in the summer, and your bush will keep shapely and tidy.

Now what about that little bit of rock garden, or the much-reduced flower border? I won't call it herbaceous border, perhaps that is a little too ambitious in war-time. But whatever you call it, you may as well make the most of it and have a sort of flower garden in miniature by turfing out the big sprawling kinds of plants, and concentrating on the dwarfer and more compact varieties. There are plenty of pretty things you could plant now which give a wealth of summer colour, but take up very little room. A few packets of seeds of hardy annuals, for instance, can brighten up a border or a small front garden with very little trouble or expense. Marigolds, cornflowers, scarlet flax, coreopsis, escholtzias, godetias, nigella, and viscarias are only a few of the annuals which make a fine show without covering much space. You merely sow the seeds broadcast in groups or patches, rake them into the soil, and put a few short twigs among them to keep them upright. Thin them out a little if necessary, and keep the weeds down, or you might wait a bit and buy a box or two of dwarf antirrhinums, asters, stocks, and lobelias. You can even plant them in the rockery if there are any bare spaces, and you can't afford new Alpine plants. A bit unorthodox, perhaps, but what does that matter in war-time? What we are after is a few bright, cheerful flowers about the place. I consider one of the brightest and most cheerful of war-time flowers is the nasturtium, there are so many types to choose from, and they will often flourish where many flowers wouldn't grow at all. The Tom Thumb varieties can be sown between the stones at the side of a crazy path, or in any odd corner, so long as the sun can get at them, and make a lovely show.

The trailing kinds can be grown up sticks like peas and will flower all through the summer. And the double gleam hybrids look lovely trailing over a heap of stones or on the roof of the air-raid shelter. I expect some of you have lost your iron railings, and feel a bit bare with nothing but the low foundation wall left standing; why not add a few rough stones to this with pocket of soil between them and put nasturtiums in them? They will trail over the wall and look much nicer than the iron railings ever did. Of course, it isn't time yet to sow nasturtiums. May is the month for that, but keep them in mind for a bit of cheap summer colour. Obviously our greatest efforts must go into the vegetable garden this year; but with a little ingenuity, we can also have a bright and cheerful show of flowers around the house without in any way interfering with food production.

April

THE SPRING HUSTLE

THERE are so many jobs to be done just now that it is difficult to know which to tackle first. We lost a good deal of time earlier on, when we ought to have been digging and preparing, owing to severe weather, and now some of us are like the cow's tail, all behind. But that need not worry us; as I have often said before, we should never garden by dates; and if the spring happens to be late, then we must be late too. The danger with so many people is that in trying to make up for lost time, they do things in such a hurry that they only half do them. That is a great mistake; try to do everything properly and thoroughly, and if you can't get the potatoes planted on Easter Monday as usual, or the other seeds sown, never mind; get them in as soon as you can, and you'll be surprised how they catch up, and make up for lost time, and by the middle of the summer everything will be about normal again. I have often planted potatoes at the end of this month, or even early in May, and the crops have been just as good. I haven't finished digging yet, but I'm not worrying about it. It'll get done in good time, and the crops, or most of them, will perhaps be all the better for a late start.

I had hoped to get a couple of rows of early potatoes in to-morrow, but I'm not sure whether I shall manage it. I shouldn't put the maincrops in even if the ground was ready. I would rather wait till the middle of this month; so long as the potatoes are nicely sprouting, they are just as well out of the ground as in it, until it has felt the influence of the spring sun and begun to warm up a bit. I expect I shall be later than most of you, because I have recently returned to my suburban home, which was put out of action for a time, and I'm trying to restore order in a very neglected back garden. I have packed the remaining rose bushes fairly close together along the back of the border, and a few of my choicest flowering plants which I don't want to lose; and I'm digging up most of what I used to call the lawn. It consists largely of weeds, moss, and bare patches, rather than grass, so I'm burying it all rather deeply, together with an accumulation of ancient rubbish and lawn mowings which has been there since the year before last. I also discovered half a bag of finely-ground poultry manure in the shed, and that's going in too, spread lightly over the soil and forked in. It looks a bit of a pickle at the moment, but I hope to get it shipshape, and planted before the end of this month. These small surburban gardens have their limitations, what with the shade from trees and fences, and the demands they make on the soil, and the depredations of cats and birds, it's no use being too ambitious. My garden seems full of birds, starlings waddling about by the score, sparrows by the hundred, and even seagulls are on visiting terms now. We fed the birds on the lawn for years, and they don't seem to have forgotten it; they are glad to see us back again, and now they seem to think that everything we put into the garden is intended for them alone. It's a bit discouraging, I admit, and I expect a good many of you are up against the same sort of problems, but even under such conditions, there is always something in the food line which can be grown successfully. I shall cut out most of the small seeds, because I'm afraid the birds would pull out the seedlings as fast as they come up. I may try a few early carrots and round beetroots; but I shall regard them as a gamble. I am sowing a few lettuces in boxes for planting out when they are big enough; and I shall probably buy or beg a few seedling onions presently, but not many, it's too risky. I have put a couple of rows of shallots in, they should be all right, and I shall try a few peas and French beans, and a row of runners. I don't suppose it will be easy to get sticks for them, but I daresay I shall manage it somehow. I shall sow some spinach in the shady parts, and for the remainder I shall grow a batch of early potatoes, in case they get a bit scarce in the summer, and follow them with brussels sprouts and savoys, and I also hope to plant out a nice lot of tomato plants. They usually do fairly well in suburban gardens, provided the sun can shine on them. They get more shelter and protection there than on allotments, and I rather hope to get enough so that we can bottle some for the winter.

Apart from these, what I am mainly concerned about is getting the garden planted up later on with greenstuff for next winter. Tomatoes can't be planted yet awhile, of course; the end of May is soon enough for that, or even early June in the North, but we can be making preparations for them. If you have a greenhouse and are able to raise your own plants, so much the better; but you must look after them, and keep them transplanted; the worst thing that can happen to them is to leave them crowded together in the seed boxes. It is well worth while to take a little trouble over them, and pot them up singly into small pots, and then into bigger ones, so that they keep growing without checks. And don't keep them too warm, it only makes them soft and tender, and then they catch a cold when you plant them out. Give them plenty of ventilation, and all the sunlight available, and keep them as near to the glass as possible. If they are on the floor or a low stage, they will grow up lanky and thin. Whatever you are growing in the greenhouse in the way of vegetable seedlings, keep them cool, it is much better for them to grow slowly into sturdy healthy plants, than to be hurried by artificial heat. You must start now and gradually harden them off; on fine days you can put them out of doors, and let them get used to it, so that when they are planted out, it won't

6

be a violent change for them. To bring plants of any kind straight from a warm, close greenhouse and plant them out of doors is asking for trouble. It is a little early yet to start hardening off tomato plants, they should be kept indoors in a comfortable atmosphere for a bit longer yet, gradually cooling them off from the beginning of next month. If you are unable to raise your own plants, order some from a nurseryman in good time, so that when planting time comes, you will have some nice strong plants, with the first flowers already showing. You won't have so long to wait for your fruit then, and time is precious where tomatoes are concerned.

Tomatoes like sunshine and warmth, so choose the sunniest part of the garden; in front of a wall or fence facing south if you can. Then dig a trench, a foot wide, and a good foot deep, spread the soil along the sides, and leave it open to the weather. The effect of sunshine and rain on the soil will be very beneficial. Before planting, you will add a little manure and fill up the trench again, but we shall come to that later.

Tomatoes under glass, if the house is heated, ought to be growing well, and even showing flowers by this time; but if it is a cold house, without any heat at all, it is better not to be in a hurry. We may get quite severe frosts yet. I have seen indoor tomatoes cut down by frost in the middle of May before now. Of course, you can't avoid taking a certain amount of risk, but I wouldn't put tomatoes in a cold house before the end of this month, and even then you may have to protect them on cold nights. Glass alone doesn't keep much frost out, although it certainly helps, especially when there is an east wind with it, but it is advisable to have some old canvas or mats, or old lace curtains, or something of the kind, handy to put over the tomatoes, either outside or inside the glass on frosty nights. It is surprising how even an old lace curtain will keep out

158

several degrees of frost, especially if the atmosphere is dry. Indoor tomatoes like a fairly rich soil, but it must be well drained, they never succeed in sodden, water-logged soil; and I should say there are more of them killed by the waterpot than by anything else. Beginners, especially, often seem to think that water is the one thing that matters, and the more of it the better, so they keep the pots full of what can only be called wet mud, and then wonder why the poor plants won't grow in it. They need water, of course, especially when the soil is full of roots, and the plants are growing and fruiting. You are not so likely to hurt them then, so long as it can drain away. The dangerous time is during the first few weeks after potting, it is very easy to over-water then: the soil should be kept just on the moist side and no more. Let it get fairly dry, until the surface soil looks quite dry, and then fill it right up, so that it percolates right through and out at the bottom; then wait till it gets dry again. The worst thing you can do is to give a little water every day. These daily driblets keep the top of the soil wet, but it doesn't get far down, and perhaps the lower half is as dry as dust; one of the first principles of gardening under glass is to learn how and when to water. You can't do it by rule of thumb, but you can use common sense, which is the greatest asset of all. Soil for the final potting of tomatoes should consist as nearly as possible of three parts fibrous loam—what exactly is fibrous loam? It is a gardener's term for old turf or top spit which has been stacked until the grass has decayed and disappeared, and the fibre consists of the old dead roots of the turf. You may not be able to get that, but get something as near to it as you can. Very well then, three parts of loam to one part old rotten manure, such as you would get from an old mushroom or cucumber bed. If you can't get that, hop manure, old leaf-mould, or peat will do. Don't sift the soil, it is better a bit coarse, and a few lumps don't matter. A little sand should be added, to make the mixture porous and help with drainage. Then to every bushel—I expect most of you can guess a bushel, more or less—add three ounces of a good fertilizer, or one of the advertised tomato fertilizers, and a double handful of soot. A double handful of wood ashes would also do good if you have any. Tomatoes are very fond of potash, but it is difficult to get, that is why I recommend a prepared fertilizer, because it contains potash. If you use hop manure, don't use quite so much as you would ordinary manure or leaf-mould: say one part to four of loam. A light sprinkling of bone meal over the mixture will also do good, but make sure that you get it all thoroughly mixed, and that isn't so easy as you might think. You can grow tomatoes in old boxes, pots, small tubs, or anything you happen to have, or you can fix up a sort of trough on the greenhouse stage with a few boards, fill it with soil, and grow them in that. Make sure that there is plenty of drainage at the bottom, broken pots or stones will do for this. Cover these with rough lumps of old turfy soil, and then fill up with the mixture. Pot the tomatoes firmly by pressing the soil well round the roots with a blunt stick, and give them a good soaking to start them off. You can train them up strings towards the glass, but in a cold house it is better to allow only two shoots to grow on each plant, picking all the others off as they appear; when you've got six or seven good bunches of flowers or fruit on a plant, be satisfied and pinch the top out; then don't allow any more new shoots to grow. But perhaps we are getting a little ahead of ourselves, we shall probably return to the subject later on. Let us finish up with a few brief reminders.

If you have a peach tree out of doors, it is probably in flower now. You should protect the flowers on frosty nights, they are easily injured, and that means no peaches. An old lace curtain or any thin material, even old fish netting hung over the front of the tree, but not touching it, will often break the drift of frost and save the flowers. If you can get a rabbit's tail, tie it to the end of a stick and when the sun is shining lightly brush the peach blossoms with it; this will ensure a set of fruit. If you have seen big buds on the black currants, and you all know what that is, get some lime sulphur, dilute it to one part neat lime sulphur in eighteen parts of water, and spray the bushes well with it when the first leaves are about the size of a shilling. It will burn the leaves and make the bushes look sick, but they soon recover, and you will have done much to prevent the spread of the big bud mite. Plant out the sweat peas which were sown in the autumn if you haven't already done so, and pinch off the original shoot, which is usually thin and tough. A new one will shoot up from the base and give you a much better plant.

Some of those yellow flowered winter jasmines growing on walls are looking a bit untidy. The shoots can be cut back now to keep them within bounds, and a new lot will soon appear for flowering next winter. Cut down the autumn fruiting raspberries, such as Hailsham Berry, November Abundance, and about half of the Lloyd George's, right to the ground. New canes will soon grow, and bear fruit in the autumn.

CARROTS AND THINGS

I should think the weather during February and early March this year was just about as spiteful as it could be, from a gardening point of view. When the ground wasn't covered with snow or frozen hard, the east wind was enough to cut your liver out, and it seemed impossible to do anything in the garden.

It wasn't exactly the sort of weather to produce the urge to Dig for Victory, was it? But since then the sun has shone, the crocuses have bloomed, and the gardening fever has been very much in evidence, and now we are all in a hurry to make up for lost time. There is quite a lot of digging not yet finished, and some of my listeners are getting hot and bothered over it, and are wondering if they can possibly get finished in time to plant or sow anything. I am getting quite a lot of letters about it; but bless me, there is nothing to worry about at all, even if you don't finish the digging before the end of this month you will still have plenty of time to get the autumn and winter crops in, and the winter crops are much more important this year than the summer crops; so perhaps being a bit late may turn out to be a blessing in disguise. So get on with it, and get the digging finished as soon as you can, and long before the end of the summer the plot will be all a-blowing and a-growing with winter greens, potatoes, swedes, carrots, celery, tomatoes, beetroots, salads, and all the good things that really matter. By the way, last Sunday morning I saw four different men setting forth to work on their new allotments, and they all had dirty spades. Now with all the other jobs most of us are rather fussy about tools; we like sharp shears for clipping, a sharp scythe or machine for mowing, sharp saws and axes, pruning-knives and carving-knives, because we can't do the job properly unless they are sharp and in good condition; so why make an exception in the case of a spade? You can't dig comfortably if the spade is rusty and plastered up with last week's dirt; so carry a little scraper with you like the old countrymen do, and scrape the soil off now and then as you dig, and never put the spade away until you have scrubbed it clean and polished it up with an oily rag. No wonder digging is, to some people, a painful ordeal, and hard labour; it might just as easily be a pleasant recreation; sometimes, on hard and stony ground the cutting edge of a spade gets turned up and blunted, have a look at it occasionally, and, if necessary, hammer it out straight, and sharpen it with a heavy file. You'll be surprised what a difference it makes to your work. The same applies to a hoe, nine out of ten of them are too blunt to cut a weed up nicely. Keep the edge sharp and see how much easier it is.

Now let us talk about some of the different vegetables; carrots, for instance. We have been hearing quite a lot about carrots lately, and their wonderful health-giving properties, and with a little careful manœuvring we can keep the supply going nearly all the year round. In the winter we eat them as a sort of national duty, whether we like them or not, but in the summer we eat them for pleasure, for of all the early vegetables there is surely none sweeter than a dish of fresh young carrots, unless it be the first green peas, and the two go very well together, and help to make life worth living, even now. So let us have a few more carrots, the little stump-rooted varieties can be sown at intervals for another three months yet. Not too many at a time, just a single row sown once a fortnight is usually enough, unless there are a lot of you, then you can have two rows. Carrots are not a good crop for newly dug pasture land, they prefer older ground which has been cultivated for some years. I don't say you can't grow them on new land; you can, but they never seem quite so good in flavour, and they often get spoilt by wireworm, which is usually prevalent in turf. So if you have any choice in the matter, keep the carrots on the old ground, there are plenty of other good things you can grow on the new, such as potatoes, peas and beans, and the winter greens. My method of growing little carrots is perhaps not quite the orthodox way. I never thin them out for one thing. I always think thinning them attracts the fly; she smells them so much easier when they have been disturbed, and then comes and lays her eggs in the holes left by the thinning. I first fork the ground over and get a fine surface tilth, then I mix together fine bone meal and dried blood fertilizer, half and half, and sprinkle it very lightly along the rows, or where the rows are going to be. You want very little. An old sugar dredger is a useful gadget for this job, and you sprinkle the stuff as lightly as you would sprinkle rationed sugar over an apple tart. Then rake it well in with an iron rake. Next make rather wide drills with the hoe a good two inches wide, or that's how I do it, and half an inch deep, sow the seeds thinly along it, rake the soil over them, and if the soil is at all dry give them a good watering if you can manage it. Then leave them alone except for hoeing between the rows until the biggest are about the size of walnuts, or a little bigger. Then you can start pulling the big ones for use. Even if you've sown them a bit thicker than you ought to have done, it doesn't matter much. They will push and squeeze each other out of the line and get plenty big enough for summer use. Mind you, these young carrots must be regarded as one of the luxury vegetables just now, and we mustn't grow too many of them at the expense of the winter store. Carrots grown for the winter are a different matter; for one thing, the varieties are different, although you *can* grow the stump-rooted kinds for storing; if you space them out well they make quite big roots, but I don't think the quality is quite so good as the longer varieties. I grew one of the stump-rooted sorts last summer for storing, and some of them weighed half a pound. They kept quite well in the store, but there is not much quality or flavour about them. They are rather on the coarse side too, and squeak at you when you bite them. I am not sorry to see the end of them. I would rather have long carrots for the winter. I admit they are a bit more trouble, and you need deep soil to get good results; last year we had one called Scarlet Intermediate, neither long nor short, but of excellent quality, and I should say this, or one of the intermediates, is the most suitable type of carrot for allotments, especially those which have not been deeply dug. The same applies to beetroots. I see no advantage in getting very long ones, even if the soil is deep. You can easily get them a foot long, but how many people have got a saucepan big enough to cook them in, and, as you know, you mustn't cut beetroots, or they bleed all the colour out, at least most of the varieties do, there are one or two exceptions. I shan't grow any more long ones, I think the round and intermediate types are not only more convenient in shape and size, but of better quality. But to return to these winter carrots. Nearly all gardening books and advisers tell you not to grow carrots, or beets either, for that matter, on ground which has been freshly manured with farmyard manure. I give that advice myself, very often, but let us be clear about it. Some of my listeners seem to have taken this too literally, and gone to the other extreme, trying to grow them on the poorest soil, which has never been manured at all. That won't answer. Actually, carrots and other root crops like a deeply dug soil well stocked with plant foods. The reason we avoid strong or fresh farm manure is not because the carrots object to it, but because it makes them grow too strong and coarse, and causes the roots to branch and fork, and grow coarse whiskers all over them, instead of producing the straight, clean roots which suit our purpose better. So we try to strike the happy medium—give them good soil, but not too strong a diet. The ideal soil for carrots is where the celery trench was last year. This was deeply broken up and well manured, or should have been, for the celery, and there is still enough goodness left in it to produce a nice clean crop of carrots or beet. You can add a little fertilizer before sowing, as I suggested for the early carrots, but nothing else should be necessary, unless you happen to have a little potash by you; if so, give them a sprinkle of that, but I don't suppose many of you have got any, and there is little or none to be had. Carrots for the winter store need not be sown yet. A good many people do sow them now, I admit, but if you sow them too early they often get past their best by the time you lift them in the autumn, and you find a lot of them coarse and woody and split, and not only that, by sowing them now you risk losing them by the fly. I suggest the end of May, or even the first week in June, for sowing the maincrop, and the same applies to beetroots, the fly has gone then, and the roots will be plenty big enough by the autumn, and of better quality. This crop must be sown in narrow drills, a good half inch deep, and later thinned out to at least six inches apart. You shouldn't need to start on these stored carrots till the New Year, because if you make the last sowing of the short ones a rather bigger sowing than the previous ones, about August Bank Holiday, you ought to be able to pull them fresh from the bed up till Christmas, at least you can in the South. You may not be so lucky in the North, because they might get frozen hard and covered with snow.

I didn't intend to say so much about carrots as this, you'll get tired of hearing about them, so let us change the subject and talk about beans. One listener says that something has happened to his broad beans, and wants to know if it is too late to sow some more. No, it isn't too late, but it's getting a bit risky now. For one thing, late sown broad beans usually get badly attacked by the black fly, and need a lot of attention, and for another, the pods mature in the height of summer, and the beans quickly get old and tough and very soon pass their best. The broad bean is essentially an early vegetable, and is not much appreciated when the other kinds are about. The next beans to be sown will be the dwarf French varieties. You could chance a couple of rows now in a sheltered place if you feel like a gamble. It isn't really safe to sow them till about the first of May, but it is surprising how often the earlier ones will get through and produce an early crop, especially if you can protect them a bit if a sharp frost comes. They may get cut down by a late frost, if they do, you just grin and bear it, or at least you bear it, you needn't grin, and sow some more. You won't have lost much. I am always learning something, and I've learnt something about these dwarf beans during the last two years. I have always gone off the deep end about overcrowding, and in common with most other scribes and preachers, have advised thinning these dwarf beans out to at least six inches apart. In theory it ought to give you a heavier crop, in practice it doesn't. I'm afraid I shall catch it for this, but the truth must be told. I've been watching some trials during the last two years and in nearly every case where the plants were left about two inches apart they yielded a heavier crop per row than those at six inches apart. So I am not going to thin them out quite so much in future. I daresay on poorer ground, and where you keep the beans gathered as fast as they grow, you might get a better and a longer crop at six inches apart. But if you are growing them for harvesting and drying for winter use, you needn't thin them out nearly so much, because you won't gather them green. The first pods will mature and ripen, and the later ones won't develop, so you don't get so many pods per plant as you do if you keep gathering them, therefore they won't need so much room. So give them less room if you are going to harvest and dry them, and more if you intend to gather them green in the summer.

Not many English people have acquired the taste for sweet corn or maize as we usually call it. Yet in America it is one of the most popular vegetable dishes, and I should think the food value is pretty good. Our hens always lay better on maize than on the food they get now. I know we are not hens, and don't lay eggs, but I don't see why we shouldn't have a few corn cobs in the garden, they are delicious if you catch them in the right condition, and they needn't take up any room, because you can dab an odd plant about here, there, and anywhere, even among the flowers, they are quite ornamental. Admittedly, they need a good summer to bring them to perfection, so the best plan is to get the seed sown under glass now, and plant them out in sunny positions about the middle of next month. They usually turn in just after you've finished the peas and are feeling a bit sad about it. You'll appreciate them then, some people like them even better than peas.

CELERY AND BEANS

I think we might usefully discuss one or two of the popular vegetables this afternoon, and see if we can make a better job of them than we did last year. Celery, for instance; this is one of the most popular of the winter vegetables, nearly everybody likes it, either cooked or raw, and it is not really difficult to grow; yet I should think there were more failures with celery last year than with anything else, largely, I believe, because so many people fail to understand its natural habits and requirements, and to cater for them accordingly. I always say that one of the first principles in growing any garden plant is to learn something of its natural habitat. Nature doesn't make many mistakes, and if we can find out how a plant grows in its wild state, the kind of soil, whether wet or dry, shady or sunny, and so on, we have a fairly good guide as to its cultural treatment in our own gardens. It isn't always easy, especially in the vegetable garden, because some of our vegetables are so far removed from their ancestors as to be almost unrecognizable, and have become acclimatized and been able to adapt themselves to different conditions; cross breeding of different varieties has changed many of them, not only in appearance, but also in their requirements. But

even so, they nearly always retain the principal character-
istics of their original ancestors, and these are the
gardener's most important guides in growing them. Now
celery is a native of this country and other parts of Europe;
it is therefore hardy; and yet it is practically always sown
under glass, a fact which misleads some people into thinking of it as a sub-tropical plant, and to coddle it rather
unnecessarily.

We sow a good many hardy plants under glass, not
because they need artificial heat, but because we want to
get them started earlier; so that when the spring weather
arrives, instead of having to start at the beginning from
seed, we can put out growing plants, thus saving time, or
adding a month or more to their growing season, to enable
them to grow into bigger and more mature plants by the
autumn. Also, by sowing under glass, we have a greater
measure of control over them, and are able to protect them
from adverse weather conditions, pests, and other troubles,
during their early infancy. Although the wild celery is a
native of this country, you don't find it growing everywhere. You can find wild parsnips and carrots on the hills,
in dry and sunny places, but not celery. Celery grows in
bogs, in wet ditches and swampy places; it revels in
stagnant, filthy quagmires. The wild celery, indeed, is an
objectionable plant, a semi-poisonous narcotic, and I often
think it is one of the gardener's greatest achievements to
have developed such a plant into the wholesome and
palatable celery of the garden. What induced them to
tackle it at all is something of a mystery; but they did, and
a very good job they've made of it, for the cultivated celery
has not only lost all its objectionable qualities, but is
wholesome and possesses very pronounced dietetic properties. It is a very different thing to its wild ancestor. Yet
it still retains its love of wet, unsavoury soils. Some of the
finest celery has been grown on sewage farms, where the

169

conditions just suit it; but the celery didn't suit us. I don't say that it did anyone any harm, but many people didn't fancy it, and complained about it, so the practice was stopped. Very well, having discovered this much about it, we try, in the garden, to imitate its natural conditions as nearly as possible, and cater for its requirements, but at the same time convert it to more respectable habits. In the first place we should choose the wettest part of the garden, where the soil is deep and rich, or we must do our best to make it so, by digging deeply, well manuring the lower soil, and giving plenty of water during the growing season. People often complain that their celery is tough and pithy, instead of sweet and crisp; this is nearly always due to lack of water. I have rarely seen good celery on a dry allotment where there was no water supply. At present your celery plants are growing in boxes in a greenhouse or frame, and in due course you will be digging a trench to plant them in. The trench is merely a convenience for earthing up the stems as they grow to keep them white and tender; if they remained their natural green they would be too tough to eat. It also makes watering easier. But trenches can easily be made too deep, and often are. A deep trench prevents the proper circulation of air, the disease spreads more readily. But the commonest fault of all is to dig a trench and plant the celery along the bottom of it without properly preparing and enriching the soil underneath; it won't grow well in clay, gravel, or any other subsoil. The best way is to dig a deep trench, as wide as the spade, or a little wider, and two spits deep, keeping the top soil separate from the lower. Then put a layer of old manure or rotten leaves into the bottom, and proceed to fill up with the top spit of soil, mixing with it a little good general fertilizer. Dried blood, poultry manure, fish manure, or any of the organics are excellent, so long as you don't overdo them. Hop manure is good, too, it helps to hold moisture.

Of the fertilizers in powder form, a good ounce to each yard of row is enough, and get it well mixed with the soil. Press the soil down a little as you put it in, and fill the trench up to about three inches from the top. This doesn't look a very deep trench, but there will be something for the plants to grow in, and it is better gradually to build up the soil in the form of a ridge as you earth up the stems, than to start with the plants at the bottom of a deep trench. There will be time to talk about earthing up later on; but there is just one other point. Celery is subject to a nasty disease known as rust, which appears later in the season. As far as I know, there is no cure for it, but you can keep it away by spraying the plants once a fortnight with Bordeaux mixture from the time they are planted out, or even before.

To make Bordeaux mixture, dissolve half a pound of copper sulphate in four gallons of water in a tub. Then, in a bucket, dissolve half a pound of fresh lime in one gallon; when thoroughly dissolved, pour the lime into the copper solution, stir well, and use it at once. There are also some very good copper preparations on the market, all ready to dilute with water, and these are even better, but I'm afraid the advertising rule doesn't allow me to mention them by name. This spraying not only prevents the rust disease, but it also helps to keep slugs away from the celery stems. The celery fly, which puts maggots in the leaves, must also be prevented; you can't do much once it is there, except squash them. I find one of the best things is to keep some dry soot handy and sprinkle it lightly over the plants through a sugar dredger when the leaves are damp.

I'm afraid that will have to do for celery. Next a word or two about the runner bean. This is everybody's vegetable, and grows almost as well in a London backyard or allotment as it does in a country garden. It is so easy to grow that it often doesn't get anything like the attention it deserves, for no vegetable crop responds to and repays kindly treatment better than the runner bean. You can get beans, of a sort, without much trouble, but if you want a good crop of good beans, you've got to treat them generously. The runner bean is not a native plant; it came from Mexico and South America, and, as most of you know, it can't stand frost, so we have to delay sowing and planting till the frost is over, which means that it only has our short summer to do its work in, so, in common with tomatoes and other sub-tropical vegetables, it is a distinct advantage if we can get it started under glass and thus save time.

In this country we grow the runner bean from seeds, and treat it as an annual, but it is really a perennial; and in its native climate it rests during the dry season, and when the heavy rains come, it shoots up into new growth, and no doubt the seeds which were shed in the autumn, or fall, grow up too, and in the rich warm soil, well stocked with humus and moisture, growth is very rapid and luxuriant. I've never been there, but I should think the runner bean in its wild state, rambling about and getting tangled up with everything else, must be a bit of a nuisance. Of course, gardeners have improved it tremendously since it has been in cultivation, and helped it to adapt itself more to our climate, but it still loves the conditions of its native land— deep soil, with plenty of rotting vegetation in it, a comparatively warm position, and plenty of water during the growing season. So, if you can prepare now, by digging a strip of soil deeply and burying in it plenty of rotten leaves, and farmyard manure, if you can get it, the beans will repay you a hundred fold. Meanwhile, if you can bring on plants under glass, ready for planting out about the middle of next month, you will be gaining time. If you can't do that, you can sow the seeds early next month; it isn't safe to sow them before. The commonest fault is to crowd them too closely together, it doesn't pay. If you want to see what a runner bean can do, plant one, all alone in some rich soil, give it a couple of tall poles to climb up and keep it watered and fed; it will surprise you. I used to know a gardener in the Thames Valley who made a hobby of growing runner beans, and won prizes with them all over the country. I have seen plenty of them eighteen inches long, and he used to grow some of them through lamp glasses, to keep them straight and get them longer. He trenched the ground three feet deep, with any amount of farmyard stuff in the lower half, mixed with barrow loads of old rotten lawn mowings and autumn leaves, but he always kept this well down below. Then he planted two rows of beans, five feet apart, with the individual beans a foot apart in the rows. Each bean was given a pole about ten feet long, and these were pulled over and tied together at the top to form an archway. When the plants were well under way, he spread a thick layer of old farm manure over the surface, both under the arch and for a yard outside, and about once a week, in dry weather, he put the hosepipe on and watered through the manure. He also syringed the plants in the morning and evening during the warm weather. I've seen those beans laid out in hampers like cucumbers, and he thought nothing of gathering a hundredweight a day from his two rows. You had to take your hat off when you walked under his archway or you were sure to get it knocked off by the heavy beans hanging from above. Now I'm not suggesting that you should grow them like that in war-time, very few people have either the time or the muck; but we might keep the idea in mind, as an ideal, and get as near to it as we can under our own circumstances.

Dig deeply, and put all the good stuff you can get into the lower regions, and don't dig a narrow trench for them; the roots spread out far beyond the confines of a trench.

Put the beans nine inches apart, and keep a few in reserve
to fill up gaps in case of accidents. Give each bean its own
pole, and when the plant reaches the top, nip the growing
point out. Give plenty of water during dry weather, if you
possibly can, and if you can manage weak liquid manure
instead of water, so much the better. In the autumn I
suggested that you should try keeping the old plants, and
storing the roots in dry soil just as you do with dahlias;
the soil should be moistened now to wake them up, if you
haven't already done it, and the old stocks divided up and
planted out early next month, or if they haven't started
growing, you can chance them at the very end of this
month. Dahlias and runner beans both come from Mexico,
and both respond to the same treatment, so if you are a
good dahlia grower, you ought to grow beans equally well
or even better. I seem to have said a lot about beans, but
they pay for doing well, so I hope it hasn't bored you. Just
one other point, if you have a neighbour who keeps bees,
invite him to put a hive in your garden for the summer,
and promise him a few baskets of beans in return. Bees
can make a big difference to the garden crops, not only
fruit crops but vegetables too, and although I don't
suggest that everybody should keep bees, I do suggest that
those who are really interested in them, and have the time
and inclination to look after them properly, might well
consider it. Bees can be very profitable, and if there were
more of them about, our gardens would be all the better
for their help. They are among the gardener's best friends.

APPLE BLOSSOM AND MOSQUITOES

It will soon be apple blossom time now, a very critical
time in the orchard and fruit gardens. We all like to see a
good show of fruit blossoms, and we are all hoping to get
a good crop of fruit this year to make up for last year's
rather poor effort. But it isn't enough to hope, we must do

what we can to help, for British fruit this year is going to be more valuable than ever before, and it all depends on a successful blossoming season. It is true that we can't do a great deal about it; we can't control late frosts and storms, for instance, but there are certain things which we can do. In the first place, fruit depends on the effective pollination of the blossom, a job which is largely done by bees. If there are no bees within reach of your garden or orchard, you are not likely to get nearly such a good crop of fruit. So what can you do about that? Many people are apt to think of a beehive as a sort of little honey factory, and value it accordingly, but it is far more than that, it is a colony of workers who help us to get better crops. Even if we never got an ounce of honey, it would still pay many of us, hand over fist, to keep a colony or two of bees. I would like to see bees kept in every large garden, and at the very least there ought to be a group of hives in every village. Of course, they have their drawbacks, they sometimes sting you, but not often, if you treat them properly and don't annoy them, and if they do, it isn't a very serious matter, not like wasps, for instance. It's a serious matter for the bee, though, because whereas a wasp can keep on stinging, I believe I am right in saying that a bee can sting only once, and it usually kills it. So it doesn't do it for the fun of the thing. I remember, years ago, when I was working under glass where we had bees to pollinate the flowers for seed purposes, I worked with them crawling all over my bare arms for hours at a time. Sometimes I got a sting, when a bee got pinched or trapped or something, but I merely pulled out the sting, rubbed it, and forgot all about it. I don't think the stinging question need prevent anyone from keeping bees. A greater drawback is that they need understanding and looking after properly. It is no use just putting a hive in the garden and neglecting them. That is why I would never advise all and sundry to keep them, but only those who are interested in them, and prepared to treat them kindly. A colony of bees can become a most fascinating hobby, as well as a profitable one, so it is well worth thinking over. If you don't fancy keeping your own, there is nearly always a beekeeper not very far away, who is only too glad to get a change of hunting-ground for his colonies, and it is usually possible for the gardener to come to some arrangement with the beekeeper, which will be to their mutual advantage. Last summer a beekeeper from a neighbouring village approached me to see if I could find accommodation for a few hives, and offered to give me honey as a sort of rent. The bees never caused the least inconvenience to any one, except that they took rather too keen an interest in the jam making, and came in to have a look, and a taste. Anyway, I am convinced that there are not enough bees in the country, and if more people realized their value and kept a few, our gardens and orchards would be very much better for it.

But to return to the fruit trees; at the moment they look quite promising, and if the weather behaves itself, and the bees do their job, we should get a good set of fruit, and this sometimes means a rather serious tax on the energy of the trees. Indeed, I have known the blossoms to set so freely on under-nourished trees that they have been unable to develop properly, and the result has been a poor crop instead of the promised abundance, the little apples dropping off by the hundreds. This can often be avoided by giving the trees a spring tonic to tide them over the critical period. Sulphate of ammonia is quite good, it can be spread over the ground under the trees now, at the rate of one ounce to each square yard, as near as you can work it out, and raked into the soil. If there is grass under the trees, it should be spread over it and watered in. Of course, you've got to use your discretion on a job like this, and only give it to the trees that need it—oldish trees that are crowded with spurs and blossom buds will benefit by it, but younger ones, on well-cultivated garden soil, which are making strong growth, but not overburdened with fruit spurs, are better without it. When you are feeding trees, remember that the feeding roots spread out quite as far as the branches, so it is no use putting it just round the main trunk; as a rule, there are no feeding roots at all there.

There is another point worth mentioning again. Many varieties of fruit trees are sterile to their own pollen, and need flowers of a different variety to cross-pollinate them, and produce fruit. This is particularly so with plums and cherries. If there are several different varieties in the same garden and plenty of bees about, all will be well, but a solitary tree, however full of blossom, may easily be quite barren of fruit. I dealt with this subject at some length not so long ago, but I am still getting enquiries as to why the one and only cherry or plum tree has plenty of blossom but no fruit. The remedy, of course, is to plant other varieties, but that takes time, and the only suggestion I can make for this year is that when the tree is in flower you get a few flowering sprays from another tree of different variety, and fix them in your tree with the stems in bottles of water. The bees will do the rest. It is no business of mine where you get the flowering branches. Wild varieties would do, but good gardening neighbours can often do a little bartering, and I think the majority of garden trees could easily spare a few sprays of blossom without missing it. It would even do them good to thin them out a bit, and if it means turning a barren tree into a fruitful one, it is surely worth the little trouble involved. But don't get breaking branches off strangers' trees and say I told you to, some people are a bit touchy about that sort of thing, and, of course, it is no good doing it until the flowers are out, and it should be done when the sun is shining.

Look out for little green caterpillars on the apple trees;

177

if you sprayed them well in the winter with tar-oil wash there shouldn't be any, but a lot of you didn't, so you had better be on the watch now, for once these caterpillars get going they can soon reduce the tree to a rather pathetic condition. They are not often noticeable till after the blossom, but you can never be sure. If you see any, spray the trees thoroughly with derris insecticide, or with arsenate of lead paste, half a pound dissolved in ten gallons of water. These washes cover the young leaves, and poison the little caterpillars when they start feeding. For amateurs I would rather recommend derris because it is non-poisonous, whereas arsenate of lead, although very effective, contains arsenic, and is poisonous to bees. So don't use it before blossoming, and don't use either or any other spray while the blossoms are open, because of the danger to bees. I have never known derris to do any harm to bees, the bees wouldn't touch it. No doubt if it were sprayed directly on to a bee it would injure it, but that is hardly likely to happen unless you sprayed it while the bees were active on the open flowers, and no sensible gardener would do that. The arsenate of lead is different, because it remains on the trees, and particles get dissolved in little globules of water, and the bees get thirsty and drink it. I have often used arsenate of lead myself, but I would never use it till well after the blooming period. There's one exception to the rule about spraying open flowers, and that is in the case of raspberries. You all know what unpleasant things maggoty raspberries are; they are put there by a little beetle which feeds on the open flowers, and also lays eggs in them, and the only way you can get at her is by spraying or dusting the open flowers. I have often dusted the open raspberry flowers with derris powder, but I have never seen a bee settle on a flower after the dusting, although I have watched carefully, nor have I ever found a dead one there. Talking of apple blossom, there is one pest which sometimes causes considerable damage without being very conspicuous. This is the apple blossom weevil, a little beetle which attacks the unopened blossoms when they are just showing pink. She makes a hole through the petals and pokes an egg right into the centre of the flower. This hatches, and the grub eats the centre of the flower, which does not open, but remains capped over like a little brown ball. If you pull it off you can often find the little white grub inside. These beetles can lay anything up to 50 or 60 eggs, so if there are plenty of them they can soon reduce the number of blossoms, and if there are not many flowers on a tree, they may ruin the crops. In many cases they merely thin out the blossoms, which doesn't matter much, and they pass unnoticed, but they can become a serious pest, and they seem to be on the increase, so you would be well advised to keep an eye open for them. They are not easy to deal with. One way of preventing them is to spray the buds all over with rather thick limewash as soon as they begin to show pink, this prevents egg laying. If you notice, at blossoming time, that large numbers of the flowers have turned brown instead of opening, a good plan is to spread sheets or something under the tree, then shake or jar the branches, the dead blossom and the grubs fall off quite easily and you can then gather them up and punish them, they won't be there next year then, to increase and multiply.

Another pest we must look out for is the aphis on the plum trees. This is a form of greenfly which curls up the leaves and makes the trees look very sorry for themselves, and once it is curled up in the leaves you can't do much about it, so have a look at the young leaves, and if you find a few little flies about spray the trees at once with derris or nicotine wash, or you may soon find your trees in a nasty mess. Here again, if you use tar-oil wash in the winter, you shouldn't be troubled, but did you?

179

While we are on the subject of pests, there is another one which is common to many gardeners in the summer, and that is the mosquito. I get a good many letters about this spiteful enemy, which drives some of my lady friends to distraction, or at least out of the garden, and I myself have often had bumps as big as sixpences on my ankles which kept me awake all night scratching and rubbing. Perhaps the worst are these little beasts that come buzzing around after your blood on a warm summer evening, when you are trying to get ten minutes rest after your labours. Some people say they never get bitten at all, so presumably even mosquitoes are discriminating in their tastes, but they seem to like the flavour of most of us. I have lately received a Ministry of Health sixpenny publication about these blood-sucking creatures, and I am surprised to find that there is such a large number of different kinds, and some of their names are as alarming as their habits. Fancy getting bitten by a Tueniorhynchus Coguilettidia Richiardii! Enough to make you careful, isn't it? Anyway, what it all boils down to is this, these creatures breed in water, mainly stagnant pools, swamps, puddles, ditches, water-butts, or any dead water which may be lying around. So the first thing is to do away with as many of these places as possible anywhere within reach of the garden. In the ornamental lily pond a few goldfish or other fancy fish will eat them while they are maggots, but a small pond without fish may be the breeding place of thousands, especially if it happens to be a shady pool. Plenty of light and cleanliness indoors, and especially in pigsties and cowsheds and such places are other ways of keeping them down. And the covering up of water-butts and other vessels containing liquids with a light-fitting lid will do much to prevent breeding. The booklet gives other remedies and preventives which are perhaps a little beyond the amateur gardener. But here is a lotion which may interest the ladies. Mix together three parts oil of citronella, two parts liquid paraffin, four parts cocoa-nut oil, and just a dash of carbolic acid. Rub this over your neck and ankles, and the mosquitoes will pass you by in disgust. I don't know whether you can get these things just now or not, so please don't blame me if you can't. You wouldn't want much anyway.

Earlier on I suggested spraying the apple trees with derris or dusting them with derris powder after the blossoms have all fallen, if you happen to see caterpillars about. Perhaps I ought to amend that, and say do it whether you see caterpillars or not, because it may also prevent egg laying by the apple sawfly and prevent a crop of maggoty apples. The sawfly lays an egg on the tiny developing apple, the maggot hatches out, gets into the apple, grows up with it, and is often there to greet you when you take the first bite in the autumn. So it is well worth while to try and prevent the eggs being laid.

May

THE LOCAL SHOW

In connection with the Dig for Victory campaign a great many local allotment and gardening societies have been formed, which is all to the good, because we can do so much more collectively than we can individually, and I for one would like to see a horticultural society in every parish in the country. Now a great many of these new societies seem to be flirting with the idea of holding a war-time vegetable and flower show during the summer, and having little or no experience of such matters, the would-be organizers are writing to me for guidance and advice. I do not claim to be an authority on shows, but I have been mixed up with a few, and there can be no harm in discussing the subject for a few minutes, and giving my opinions for what they are worth.

The first point to consider is whether or not we are justified in holding a show this year? There are, of course, objections and many difficulties to be got over, such questions as transport, petrol restrictions, the time occupied in organizing it, refreshments, and so on. And then many people maintain that a show is a waste of time, and that the men would be better employed in their gardens and allotments, that the expense is unjustified, and that to introduce the holiday atmosphere which is usually associated with a local show is quite wrong and unpatriotic in times like these, and what good does it do anyway?

On the other side of the argument there is also a good deal to be said in favour of a show, even in war-time. Consider the position of the local society first. I think we are all agreed as to the advantages and the usefulness of a well-organized society in the food production scheme; seeds, fertilizers, and other supplies can be bought collectively and cheaply. Technical knowledge and other resources can be pooled, and so on. I don't think there is any need to go into details about the benefits and the good work which can be done by men and women grouped together for mutual assistance as against the individual who ploughs his lonely furrow.

Now I have had a good deal of experience in the forming of local societies, and I have nearly always found that it is a comparatively easy matter to start a society. You get plenty of initial support and often a great wave of enthusiasm at the first meeting, and everybody seems as keen as mustard about it. But it is quite another matter to keep it alive after the first few months when the novelty wears off and the men begin to lose interest. They must be kept together, their interest and enthusiasm must be kept alive by regular meetings, or by some other method which will prevent that apathy and a quiet petering out which is the fate of so many local societies. How often have I been told, "It's no use trying to do anything like that here, they don't take any interest. We've started things before, but they never last long." Why? Simply, I suspect, because no effort is made to keep them alive. The local gardening and allotment society then must have some inducement in it to keep the members active and interested, and I should think the greatest of these inducements is the annual show. It is the climax of a successful season, the gathering of the clans, the great day of reckoning when the members can compare results, enter into friendly arguments, and show each other what they really can do.

Gardeners love to swank a bit and to go one better than their neighbours. I may have told you the story of the man who, in his suburban garden, had an oil barrel standing on end close to the dividing fence, cunningly concealed by bushes. On the barrel was a tub of rich soil, and in this grew an outsize hollyhock. When a friend asked him what the idea was he said quietly, "That's for the benefit of the chap next door; he beat me by a foot last year," which goes to show to what lengths that spirit of competition will lead a man if he hasn't the safety-valve of a local show to enable him to indulge it legitimately.

The show creates tremendous local interest in gardening, and is a direct inducement to a higher standard of cultivation. Moreover, in these days shows are usually organized with a double object, to encourage more and better food production, and to assist charities. The Red Cross benefited substantially last year from the proceeds of local shows, and hopes to do still better this year.

So I for one am definitely in favour of holding a local show wherever it can be done without interfering in any way with the war effort generally.

Having decided to hold a show, the next thing to settle is the most suitable date. Obviously the most attractive month is July, when we get the warm weather and the long evenings, and if flowers were the first consideration there would be very little argument about it.

But this year vegetables are the first consideration and from a food production point of view July is not a suitable time, because most vegetables are not ready, and we certainly don't want to see men digging up two or three rows of potatoes or other vegetables just to find a dozen good ones, that means waste, and we must do everything possible to avoid waste in any shape or form. Therefore it is better to wait till the normal harvesting season, and I suggest sometime during September, or if it is to be held in the village hall or entirely under cover, you could make it October. The ideal show, of course, is the outdoor one with a tent or two and the usual side-shows and sports, and early September is a good time for that. There is still enough warmth and daylight to justify it, and most of the crops are ready then. The next thing is to appoint a small show committee to work out details and get on with it. There are many purely local questions which can only be decided on the spot, whether you have it in the gardens of the local mansion, or the village hall, or a farmer's barn is for you to settle. You will be up against all sorts of difficulties, and there will always be local Jeremiahs to throw cold water on every suggestion, but don't heed them.

Last year we decided to hold our show in the grounds of the local mansion, a lovely setting. We were told by the wiseacres that we couldn't possibly get a marquee, the Army had commandeered them all, and if we could get one we shouldn't be allowed to put it up. But we did get one and we did put it up, or at least the makers did. There was no possible hope of getting a band in war-time, but we did get one, a Home Guard Band, and a jolly good one too. Gradually we got over each obstacle in turn, not without a few struggles, but the show was an outstanding success from every point of view, and preparations are now under way for an even better one. The difficulties will be greater this year, especially where transport and light refreshments are concerned, but it is surprising how you can get over or around them if you make up your minds, and don't be too ready to take "no" for an answer.

There is just one tip I would like to give to local organizers, go and see your local police superintendent and tell him all about it. He may prove very helpful and prevent you inadvertently committing some technical offence, and it is much better to keep on the right side of the police, and get permission for what you do, than to have the local constable walking into your show and saying, " You can't do that there here."

Next, you will have to prepare a schedule or programme; this is an important item and requires a good deal of care. You must draw up your rules for the show, dates of entry, times of staging and removal, and so on, and make everything very clear and straightforward so that no one can misunderstand it. You can usually borrow from some other good society a specimen, which will help you to keep on the right lines. Set out the classes clearly and say exactly what you mean in every case, a badly or vaguely worded schedule can often lead to disqualifications, and nobody likes to be disqualified through having made a simple mistake. Try to avoid all ambiguous terms, sometimes you see classes for hardy herbaceous perennials, half-hardy annuals, biennials, and so on, and a good many amateurs come a cropper over them. In war-time it is better to have just a few simple flower classes only, such as a vase of garden flowers, grown entirely out of doors, or flowers grown from seed this year, or just a vase of sweet peas or roses, without a lot of confusing ideas. In the vegetable classes state the exact number of each to be shown, or the space allowed, and be very careful how you use the words "kinds" and "varieties"; six kinds of vegetables is not the same as six varieties of vegetables. Potatoes, peas, and onions are different "kinds" of vegetables. King Edward, Majestic, and Sharpe's Express are varieties of potatoes. Bedford Champion and Ailsa Craig are varieties of onions, and so on. If you think certain vegetables should be washed, or shown complete with tops, such as spring-sown onions or carrots, say so in the schedule; spend a little time over every class and get it worded so that there can be no misunderstanding it, for you must remember that whatever appears in the schedule is binding on judges, officials, and exhibitors alike. You can't alter it on the day of the show and say you meant something different.

It is rather nice, if the printer can undertake it, and get the paper, to have a nice little souvenir programme and schedule combined with a few notes and articles and illustrations in it, then you can sell it in aid of the funds. We made a good profit on ours, the advertisements more than paid for it. Get your committee together and work out the various duties, so that each man knows exactly what his job is when the day comes. You don't want to be falling over each other, all trying to do the same thing. You should insist on all entries being in at a specified time, a few days before the show, then when you know just how many entries are coming into each class you can mark out spaces for them on the tables, and have a steward in attendance to see that exhibitors put them in the right place.

If you possibly can, choose a stranger from outside to do the judging, it nearly always causes trouble if a local man acts as judge, the losers are sure to suspect that he knew whose stuff he was judging. Sometimes your County Horticultural adviser will take it on, or will recommend a suitable judge for you. All the local details, such as refreshments, sports, side-shows, and music, are outside my province, but you should do all you can to make the event attractive to outsiders, especially if you are out to collect as many sixpences as possible. If you decide to run the show for the benefit of the Red Cross, you can get tickets, show cards, posters, and other literature, by applying to the Red Cross Agricultural Fund, 34 Southampton St., Strand, London, W.C. 2.

Finally, invite the village policeman in and give him a pint of beer, and all will be well.

Just a word in conclusion to exhibitors themselves. In the first place, follow the rules and the wording of the schedule carefully, and don't depart from it or you may be disqualified. Remember that people will be paying to look at your exhibits, so show them as attractively as possible. A well-displayed collection of vegetables with a suitable background will always score points over an equally good collection carelessly arranged. Think of table quality in everything as the most important, mere size often means coarseness, and outsize potatoes or other vegetables are not necessarily the best. If you show a collection of vegetables, balance it properly so that it represents a well-cropped garden, not too many root vegetables with no greens, or vice versa; try to include potatoes, onions, one of the roots, one of the Brassicas, a dish of peas or beans, and so on. Don't polish or fake anything, and don't remove the stalks of tomatoes or any of the small fruits, such as raspberries. Don't curse the judges or sulk for the rest of the day if you don't get the first prize, resolve to do better next time. Gardeners are usually good sports and can take a beating as well as most people, but there are exceptions.

And so, good-bye for the present. I expect you will hear from me again in due season; but in the meantime let us all work together to make this the greatest and most successful gardening year we have ever had. Let us break down the barriers of exclusiveness and be good neighbours, and help each other all we can. Let us produce all we possibly can, and having produced it, make the best possible use of it, wasting nothing. And above all, let us keep cheerful hearts and smiling faces. We shall not get through the war any quicker, or any easier, if we go about like bears with sore heads. If we only put our backs into it, and pull together, we can look forward with every confidence.

LUXURIES

In these critical times the wise gardener is thinking of the winter supplies, and concentrating his energies on getting plenty of the utility vegetables. Potatoes, carrots, onions, parsnips, swedes, artichokes, and winter greens are of the first importance. But it doesn't follow that we should deny ourselves everything in the nature of a luxury, especially as some of the so-called luxury vegetables can be produced without interfering with the general Dig for Victory plans.

Variety is good for us, and the vegetable diet can become a little monotonous without the addition of an occasional novelty, just by way of a change, and to add interest to the proceedings. Apparently a good many of my listeners have been thinking along these lines, for I have had quite a lot of letters lately about such things as mushrooms, melons, and pumpkins: to say nothing of asparagus, peaches, and strawberries.

Now I am not going to advocate the growing of any of these in war-time if it means neglecting the essential subjects; but where they can be conveniently fitted into the scheme of things, to add variety, and make life a little more worth living, I'm all for them, in moderation, of course. Take mushrooms, for example. Many a savoury dish can be lifted from the mediocre to the sublime by the addition of a mushroom or two; but we can't all afford to pay seven shillings a pound for them, so why not grow a few, or at least have a shot at it? There is no need to construct elaborate pits or sheds, or buy loads of expensive stable manure, unless you are making a serious business of it. You can have a little flutter on almost any grass patch, or even among the bushes in an odd corner, provided you regard it as a gamble and don't cry if nothing happens. You won't have lost much anyway. I grew a couple of dozen beauties under a group of shrubs, and a still better crop in a celery trench, where they appeared of their own accord. I had been trying to grow some in a dark shed in the orthodox way, where I made a bed with a couple of loads of nicely turned and seasoned stable manure, following all the rules to the letter, but nothing happened; not a smell of a mushroom did I get. The bed gradually got stale and sour and cold, and, in due course, I gave it up as a bad job, and used

7

the manure for the celery, and then the mushrooms came up, hundreds of them, all over the sides of the trench. Mushrooms are like that—rather temperamental. They grow if they think they will, but they won't be dictated to. Now let us assume that you still have a bit of lawn or a grass patch, or a paddock of grass field. All you require is a barrow-load or a few buckets of fresh horse droppings. If you are in the country you can usually manage that, if you watch your opportunities; in the towns it is not so easy (sorry to talk about such things in the middle of the rhubarb and custard, but there's no getting away from it in a garden). You also require a carton of mushroom spawn, which you can get from any good seedsman. Get the sterilized spawn, if you can; it is much better, but if there is none available, get a brick of ordinary spawn.

Now cut out a piece of turf, about nine inches square, and put on one side. Scoop out the soil underneath it with a trowel to make a hole six inches deep or rather more; fill this with horse manure, and make it fairly firm; then into the middle of this press a piece of mushroom spawn about the size of a walnut, and, finally, replace the turf and tread on it. You can make these holes a couple of feet apart all over the grass. Or if you do it in odd corners among the bushes where there is no turf, you merely cover it with a good inch of soil. Do this any time during the next month and then forget all about it. Perhaps nothing will happen, but, on the other hand, given favourable weather, by the end of August or early September, you may find mushrooms bobbing up all over the place, and then, of course, you will have to stop mowing the grass or using the hoe. You can also grow mushrooms in a cold frame, after you have finished raising seedlings in it. Only for this purpose you should move it into the shade, at the north side of the building, or somewhere like that, away from the hot sun. If it is a shallow frame, you will have to dig the soil out from under it for a foot or so to give sufficient depth. Get a load of fairly fresh stable manure which hasn't been out in the rain; it doesn't matter if there is a fair amount of straw with it, and if you've got a heap of dead leaves, mix them with it, about a third of the leaves to two-thirds stable manure. Turn and mix it two or three times to let it ferment, and then put it in the frame and tread it down firmly till it is about a foot deep. It will be hot and steamy, so you must leave it till it begins to cool down; when it is just comfortably warm (between 70 and 80 degrees, if you test it with a thermometer), you press bits of mushroom spawn into it, nine inches apart. Then you put the lights on, but keep them wedged up at the back with a bit of wood, so that they are open about half an inch to let the hot air out, and cover them over completely with old sacks or straw or bracken to keep them dark and even in temperature. Have a look in about ten days; and as soon as you see little white threads of mycelium appearing, cover the bed with an inch of soil, and shut the frames up as before. If the bed is in good condition to start with, water shouldn't be necessary, and it is better if you can manage without, but if the soil gets dry, water it lightly with a rose-can in the morning, and leave enough ventilation to allow the moisture to evaporate. Be patient, and don't keep opening it every day to have a look. You won't get mushrooms for a month or two, and if they don't turn up trumps you won't have lost much; the manure will still be good for the garden.

Another way of using the frame in the summer is to grow melons in it. There are certain varieties of melons which grow quite well in a cold frame. Hero of Lockinge is a good one, as good as those grown in hot houses, and most well-known seedsmen offer one or two good varieties suitable for the frame, in addition to the Canteloupe varieties.

Here again a barrow-load of stable manure is an asset, because it provides warmth to give the plants a good start. It should be put in the bottom of the frame, pressed down, and covered with six inches of soil. Three or four seeds can be sown now in a group in the middle of the frame, but if you can get young plants brought on in pots ready for planting, so much the better. You must keep the lights on, but give a chink of ventilation whenever the weather allows it, and shade from the strong mid-day sun by putting an old lace curtain or something similar over the glass. As the plants grow, train a shoot towards each corner of the frame, and when they have nearly reached it, pinch out the growing point to induce branching. During hot weather the plants must be syringed well every morning, and they must be kept watered as required. Give ventilation during the day, and close the lights in the evening. When the flowers appear, they must be hand-pollinated. The simplest way to do this is to pick off a male flower, that is one with a thin stalk, tear off or roll back the petals, and dust the pollen into the centre of the female flowers, which are the ones with the tiny melon already showing below the flower, and quite easy to distinguish; they are very much like marrow flowers, only smaller. Unless this pollinating is done, there won't be any melons, so don't forget it. And when the melons begin to form, put something under them to cock them up away from the soil.

That brings us to pumpkins, but I'm not sure that pumpkins can be classed with the luxury vegetables. A good pumpkin is worth having, if you save it for the winter. You can make pumpkin pie with it, or mix it with other fruits and vegetables; it makes them go further, and absorbs the flavours, either sweet or savoury. Pumpkins are grown in the same way as marrows. You can sow the seeds out of doors now, two or three seeds in a group, and put a glass cloche over them, or a box with a pane of glass over it does quite well to protect the young plants during their infancy. When the fruits appear, put a board or a heap of brushwood under them to prevent slugs spoiling them. Give them plenty of water, and something a little stronger if necessary, and you should have no difficulty in getting a few good pumpkins.

Nearly everyone likes to grow a few marrows, and it seems to be generally understood that the only place to grow vegetable marrows is on a muck heap. The marrow is certainly a very useful plant for covering up an unsightly heap, but it will grow just as well on the flat ground, provided there is some good soil for it to grow in, for marrows have a lot to do in a short time and they need plenty of nourishment. Last year I suggested covering the Anderson air-raid shelters with marrow plants. Most of these are covered with soil, and resemble a mound of earth which needs keeping out of sight. But I was surprised to find that a large number of people, in following this advice, planted the marrows on the top of the shelter, where the soil was shallow, and dried out during the summer. They should, of course, be planted at the base of the mound, say a couple of plants each side in pockets of prepared soil, if necessary, with some good manure mixed with it. Then they won't get so dry, and the shoots can be trained over the shelter as they grow. I always think marrows are better if the shoots are trained over something, even if you have to build some sort of rough framework for them. It allows air to circulate round the fruits, and keeps them off the ground and away from slugs and other troubles. When there is nothing to train them over, and where space is limited, the bush varieties are more suitable; these make a compact plant which does not spread about, and can, therefore, be planted at the corners of the plot, or where there wouldn't be room for the wandering kinds. Seeds can be sown out of doors now, but it is advisable to protect them in their early days by putting a small hand light or bell glass over them. I use a box with the bottom knocked out, and a pane of glass over it. You can also sow outdoor or ridge cucumbers now. Cucumbers are likely to be scarce and expensive this year, so if you are particularly fond of them you had better grow a few. The outdoor kinds are quite good in quality, if not in appearance. They are grown in the same way as marrows, except that they require very much less room. But there is one important difference; whereas marrows and melons have to be pollinated before they will set fruit, cucumbers don't. If you pollinate a cucumber, it bulges out like an Indian club and gets full of hard seeds, which spoil it from a salad point of view. It is strange that a cucumber should form its fruit without being fertilized, but it does. A marrow or a melon would just drop off without developing. Considering the way we eat cucumbers, this seems to be a very convenient and obliging habit.

I notice that potatoes are already through the soil here and there; they will have to be careful, or they may get their noses nipped. There is still plenty of time for sharp night frost, although we hope there won't be any more. But it's as well to be on the safe side, and it is quite a good idea to pull the soil over the young potato tops with the hoe, just for another week or two, in case of accidents. I haven't finished planting mine yet. I want to get two more rows of Arran Banner in, and I wouldn't mind betting a petrol coupon that they will catch up and be as good as any of the others. One of the important jobs coming on now is thinning—a job which needs to be done carefully and gently. After a shower, when the soil is wet, is the best time; the seedlings pull out easier then, without damaging those left behind. Don't throw the thinnings away; nearly all these little seedling vegetables, such as turnips, carrots, onions, lettuces, and parsnips, can be washed and used in salads. They are quite tasty and tender. Dust a little calomel dust over the onion bed, and over the other crops after thinning, to keep the flies away. Flies are very active now, and there is nothing better than calomel dust for preventing their attacks. You can get it from most horti-cultural chemists and sundriesmen. One thing I like about war-time gardening is that I have less mowing to do; there isn't much left to mow, so I get on with the hoeing instead; hoeing between the vegetable rows is a much more useful occupation, and keeps the crops on the move, so don't let the hoe get rusty.